BRIGHT NOTES

THE MAJOR POETRY OF WILLIAM WORDSWORTH

Intelligent Education

Nashville, Tennessee

BRIGHT NOTES: The Major Poetry of William Wordsworth
www.BrightNotes.com

No part of this publication may be used or reproduced in any manner whatsoever without written permission, except in the case of brief quotations in critical articles and reviews. For permissions, contact Influence Publishers http://www.influencepublishers.com.

ISBN: 978-1-645424-74-1 (Paperback)
ISBN: 978-1-645424-75-8 (eBook)

Published in accordance with the U.S. Copyright Office Orphan Works and Mass Digitization report of the register of copyrights, June 2015.

Originally published by Monarch Press.
John W. Elliott, 1965
2020 Edition published by Influence Publishers.

Interior design by Lapiz Digital Services. Cover Design by Thinkpen Designs.

Printed in the United States of America.

Library of Congress Cataloging-in-Publication Data forthcoming.
Names: Intelligent Education
Title: BRIGHT NOTES: The Major Poetry of William Wordsworth
Subject: STU004000 STUDY AIDS / Book Notes

CONTENTS

1)	Introduction to William Wordsworth	1
2)	The Reverie of Poor Susan	20
3)	We are Seven	22
4)	The Thorn	25
5)	Simon Lee	31
6)	Lines Written in Early Spring	35
7)	To My Sister	38
8)	Expostulation and Reply	41
9)	The Tables Turned	45
10)	Strange Fits of Passion Have I Known	50
11)	She Dwelt Among the Untrodden Ways	52
12)	I Travelled Among Unknown Men	54

13)	Three Years She Grew in Sun and Shower	56
14)	A Slumber Did My Spirit Seal	59
15)	Lucy Gray	61
16)	The Two April Mornings	65
17)	The Fountain	68
18)	The Old Cumberland Beggar	71
19)	Michael	76
20)	Resolution and Independence	87
21)	The Solitary Reaper	98
22)	To the Cuckoo	103
23)	My Heart Leaps Up When I Behold	107
24)	To the Small Celandine	110
25)	To the Same Flower	123
26)	To the Daisy	126
27)	I Wandered Lonely as a Cloud	129
28)	Tintern Abbey	132
29)	Ode: Intimations of Immortality from Recollections of Early Childhood	152

30)	What Critics Have Thought of the Work of William Wordsworth	171
31)	Essay Questions and Answers	178
32)	Bibliography	186

INTRODUCTION TO WILLIAM WORDSWORTH

EARLY LIFE AND FORMAL SCHOOLING

William Wordsworth was born April 7, 1770 in a small Cumberland village named Cockermouth, located on the northern edge of the Lake District. He was the second of five children born to John and Anne Wordsworth. The family lived in a stately home near that "fairest of all rivers," the Derwent, and across the River from their home was one of William's favorite places, Cockermouth Castle, settled into ruins.

INFANT SCHOOL

Along with Mary Hutchinson, who was to become his wife in 1802, Wordsworth attended infant school at Penrith. The school was taught by Anne Birkett, about whom Wordsworth wrote some thirty years later - she "did not affect to make theologians, or logicians, but she taught to read, and she practised the memory."

RURAL EXPERIENCES

From Penrith Wordsworth moved to grammar school in the small town of Hawkshead, located in one of the most beautiful regions of the Lake District. He remained at Hawkshead until he was sixteen, studying under William Taylor and living in the home of a village dame, Anne Tyson, for whose kindness and fostering Wordsworth expressed great gratitude in *The Prelude*. Of the Reverend Taylor, Wordsworth spoke affectionately: "an honored teacher of his youth, a faithful guide, a lover of the poets." The days that Wordsworth spent at Hawkshead were among the most important in his life. Besides the serious study that he did there, and there is reason to think that he encompassed broad areas of literature, there were the long and deeply impressive rambles through the country. The first books of Wordsworth's long autobiographical poem, *The Prelude,* reveal the profound way that these early experiences at Hawkshead, walking, trapping, nutting, shaped his life.

COLLEGE DAYS

When Wordsworth's father died in 1783, his uncles became his guardians. When his Hawkshead school days ended in 1787, they sent him to Cambridge, to attend St. John's College. He was not particularly excited by the course of study there, but he proceeded through the requirements and took his B.A. degree in January of 1791. Not unexpectedly, given his former interests and directions, the greatest stimulation of the Cambridge days was from his experiences with nature. Books III and VI of *The Prelude* tell how Wordsworth "As if awakened, summoned roused, constrained, / . . . looked for universal things; perused / The common countenance of earth and sky. . . ." But during the first summer vacation in 1788, he returned to the sights and sounds of the Hawkshead region. It was during this time, recounted in Book IV of *The Prelude*, that he vowed himself a dedicated spirit:

I made no vows, but vows Were then made for me; bond unknown to me Was given, that I should be, else sinning greatly, A dedicated Spirit.

Accompanied by his sister, Dorothy, who was to enrich his life more than is easily told, and by Mary Hutchinson, Wordsworth spent the second summer vacation (1789) wandering through the country of Derby and York. Robert Jones was his companion for a walking tour in the summer of 1790 through the countries of France, Switzerland, and Italy. He was deeply moved by his meetings with the people of France, but he was more deeply moved by the Alpine scenery.

WORDSWORTH'S STAY IN FRANCE

After taking his degree from St. John's College, Wordsworth was in London for several months, toured the northern parts of Wales with his Welsh friend, Robert Jones, and departed for France in November, 1791, with the idea of learning French in preparation for becoming a tutor. Wordsworth developed passionate sympathies with the cause of the French Revolution, thinking it a great movement for the liberation of man from dehumanizing forces. Wordsworth was in Orleans in the early days of December. He tells in *The Prelude* of his meeting with Michel Beaupuy, a Republican general, with whom he discoursed often about the end Of civil government, and its wisest forms; Of ancient loyalty, and chartered rights, Custom and habit, novelty and change; Of self-respect, and virtue in the few For patrimonial honour set apart, And ignorance in the labouring multitude.

Wordsworth's natural predispositions to democracy were stirred by his friendship with Beaupuy, and he found himself more and more involved in social and political concerns. He was to ride the wave of French Republicanism through the following six years, finding himself at the end gravely disappointed.

RETURN TO ENGLAND

But the most important event of Wordsworth's sojourn in France was his relationship with Annette Vallon, who bore him a daughter in December, 1792. There is good reason to think that Wordsworth and Annette intended marriage, but their relationship was interrupted by a summons that Wordsworth received from his uncles announcing that he was to return to England immediately; they had become alarmed at his growing revolutionary sympathies. Since he was entirely dependent upon them for support, he did not have much choice in the matter. Before they called him home to England, Wordsworth had made plans to return home to ask their permission for his marriage with Annette. Any return to France was made impossible by the English declaration of war against France in February of 1793. The year that followed the declaration of war was one of torture for the poet. Besides all the emotional tumult he experienced after leaving Annette behind in France with his daughter Caroline, he had not only his failing hopes for the Revolution to deal with, but also near ostracism from his family. Wordsworth was not to see Annette again until 1802.

THE ALFOXDEN DAYS AND LYRICAL BALLADS

Two of Wordsworth's poems had been published in 1793, "An Evening Walk," and "Descriptive Sketches." These poems depart little from traditional 18th-century literary practices. The following year was not poetically productive. Wordsworth had tried to quicken his stride in 1793 and 1794 by sharing social and political concerns with such radicals as William Godwin, by whom he was greatly influenced, Tom Paine, and Mary Wollstonecraft. There were also activities of a more muscular sort-walks over a sizable expanse of English soil. One may date Wordsworth's recovery of spirit roughly from October of 1795. During this year he experienced the quickening of his interest in nature through the ministry of his sister's poetic eye; he also met Samuel Taylor Coleridge, although their friendship was not to come full fruition until about a year and a half later. Wordsworth read a good deal during these months, but the most impressive and abiding influences were supplied by the country around Racedown. There can be no question about the value of the association of brother and sister for Wordsworth's growth as a poet; he recognizes the blessing and gives thanks for it often in his poetry. Dorothy possessed an extraordinary gift of acute perception and revealing description. A passage from one of her letters written during the Racedown residence reveals the tone of those days:

We are now surrounded with winter prospects without doors, and within have only winter occupations, books, solitude and the fireside; yet I may safely say we are never dull. . . .

Coleridge visited with the Wordsworths at Racedown during June of 1797. This was the beginning of one of the most mutually productive friendships in the history of literature. In July the Wordsworths were the guests of Coleridge for two weeks at Nether Stowey. The most vivid testimony to the deep relationship between Wordsworth and Coleridge is the fact that the Wordsworths moved only weeks later into a spacious dwelling at Alfoxden, a beautiful area of country located only three miles from the site of the Coleridge home. For the year following, the Wordsworths and Coleridge (Mrs. Coleridge was not so interested) were very nearly constant companions. They went on long walks together, shared an intense enthusiasm for nature, talked about poetry for long hours, discussed ideas, issues, feelings, all of which found literary focus in the planning and writing of a volume of poems, titled *Lyrical Ballads,* first published in 1798. Some of the more well-known poems by Wordsworth that appeared in this volume are "Simon Lee," "We Are Seven," "The Thorn," "Expostulation and Reply," and "Tintern Abbey." Coleridge's famous poem "The Rime of the Ancient Mariner" was the first poem in the volume. One of the best sources of information - perhaps the best - for studying the Alfoxden days in Wordsworth's life is Dorothy Wordsworth's Journal, rich in its report of the intimate feelings of the "three persons with one soul." Wordsworth and Coleridge agreed that they would each write the kind of poems for which they were best suited; each man had his own particular job to do.

When *Lyrical* **Ballads** was published in October of 1798, the Wordsworths were settling into residence in the German town of Goslar for the four coldest and most homesick months of their lives. The trip to Germany had begun in the middle of September. The Wordsworths and Coleridge had undertaken the journey for intellectual purposes, chiefly to learn the German language. Coleridge went on to Gottingen to study; the Wordsworths spent as much time as the weather would allow touring the country. Although it was a predominantly wretched time for Wordsworth, he wrote some of his most famous poetry, including "Nutting," "Ruth," parts of *The Prelude,* and the *Lucy Poems.*

THE SECOND EDITION OF LYRICAL BALLADS

In May of 1799 the Wordsworths joyously returned to England, and began looking for a place to live. After visiting with the family of Mary Hutchinson, Wordsworth went on a walking tour through the Lake Country, accompanied by his brother, John Wordsworth, Coleridge, and Joseph Cottle, the publisher of *Lyrical Ballads*. Wordsworth wished particularly to share the area of his former home with Coleridge, and he wanted to look for a suitable place for him and his sister to live. On 20 December the Wordsworths moved into a cottage that the poet had located in Grasmere; Dove Cottage at Townend was to be their home until 1808.

The following year, 1800, proved to be one of the most productive in Wordsworth's life. With Coleridge he planned the second edition of the *Lyrical Ballads;* the work was to be issued in two volumes. During the year Wordsworth finished the first and second books of *The Prelude,* he worked on the huge work that was to remain a fragment, *The Recluse,* he wrote *The Brothers*, "Michael," "Hart-Leap Well," and a number of other poems. The year is particularly memorable for the writing of the famous "Preface" to the second edition of *Lyrical Ballads*. It contains Wordsworth's own statement of his poetic credo.

A LAPSE, A GROWTH, A DYING-AWAY

The year that followed the preparation of the second edition of the *Lyrical **Ballads*** was for Wordsworth poetically unproductive. There was during this year an important three-month visit of Mary Hutchinson at Dove Cottage; there was continued involvement with Coleridge; there was the unsettled tension between faith in France and his own deep loyalty to Britain; there was the abiding love of his sister for him, from whose unflagging devotion he continued to draw spiritual nourishment and poetic inspiration.

NEW CREATIVITY

But the passing of a year brought a renewal of creative strength. In 1802 and 1803 Wordsworth wrote nearly forty poems, including such favorites as "My Heart Leaps Up," and "The Solitary Reaper." During 1802 he began work on one of his most famous poems, "Ode: Intimations of Immortality." He expanded the first "Preface" for *Lyrical Ballads,* and prepared for publication an Appendix on "Poetic Diction." But *Lyrical* **Ballads** received much more blame than praise. Through these years of high productivity, Wordsworth was encouraged and strengthened through his friendship with Coleridge. Although there were some basic differences of belief regarding what poetry is and should do, the two poets were close friends and were much concerned about each other's work. But Wordsworth was the more productive of the two, and there is reason to believe that his worry over Coleridge's failing health and relationships warmed his poetry during the seven years following the turn of the century.

In August of 1802, Wordsworth and his sister traveled to France to meet with Annette and Caroline. They spent the month in Calais, during which time Wordsworth and Annette enjoyed amiable relations; Wordsworth gave Annette a yearly sum for the support of Caroline. The time in France was immortalized by Wordsworth's beautiful **sonnet**, "It is a Beauteous Evening."

MARRIAGE

Upon returning to England Wordsworth asked Mary Hutchinson to be his wife, and they were married October 4, 1802. Between 1803 and 1808 four children were born to them in Dove Cottage at Grasmere. Other important events in Wordsworth's life during these years included the establishment of a friendship with Sir George Beaumont, which continued until Beaumont's death in 1827, and the shocking news of the drowning of Wordsworth's brother John in the sinking of the Abergavenny, 5 February. Out of the experience was written Wordsworth's famous "Elegiac Stanzas," a poem that is much read for what it shows of the poet's changing view of the world. A number of poems were published in 1807 in Poems in Two Volumes.

When Wordsworth moved with his growing family to Allan Bank in 1808, the production of poems of great spirit was past. Wordsworth finished "The Excursion" at Allan Bank, and he continued writing poetry for the rest of his life, but the great poems were written in the Grasmere days and before.

By 1811 there were five children in the Wordsworth family, and there was another move, this time to the parsonage near the Grasmere church. The years that followed the close of Wordsworth's period of great productivity were for a number of reasons saddening years. Included in the misfortunes of the time was an estrangement from Coleridge in 1810, for which neither of the poets was truly responsible. Wordsworth made the final move of his life in 1813.

He made his residence at that time at Rydal Mount, the home that was to become his favorite of all the places he had lived.

THE SETTLED CONSERVATIVE

The eleventh book of *The Prelude* shows a serious bend in the road toward settled conservatism, away from the passionate expression of republican sympathies that had marked his life to that time. The life that Wordsworth lived at Rydal Mount has been spoken of as a "model of domesticity." He enjoyed the solicitous attentions of both his sister Dorothy, and his wife. He received a great number of visitors, to whom he read from his own poetry and with whom he discussed literature in a more general way. In 1812 he made a trip to London and became reconciled during that time with his old friend, Coleridge. In 1814 he made the first of a rather large number of tours that he would enjoy with family and friends. The University of Oxford bestowed an honorary degree upon him in 1839, and in 1843 he succeeded Robert Southey as Poet Laureate.

After enjoying seven years of the Laureateship, Wordsworth died 23 April 1850, and was buried in Grasmere churchyard.

CONTEMPORARY CRITICS

Robert Southey said of Wordsworth's achievement, "Every year shows more and more how strongly Wordsworth's poetry has leavened the rising generation." Thomas De Quincey in 1835 surveyed Wordsworth's changing reputation in these words: "Up to 1820 the name of Wordsworth was trampled underfoot; from 1820 to 1830 it was militant; from 1830 to 1835 it has been triumphant."

THE LYRICAL BALLADS

Before writing the *Lyrical Ballads,* Wordsworth had tried his hand at several other poems, although today we read such early poems as "An Evening Walk" and "Descriptive Sketches" mainly because they are interesting examples of a poet's work in the early stages of his development. These two examples of the early poetry show Wordsworth composing in the established tradition of eighteenth-century poetry. They are not really representative of the Wordsworth we usually read.

PLAN

The plan of the *Lyrical **Ballads*** was a shared effort between Wordsworth and Samuel Taylor Coleridge. This cooperative enterprise was first conceived when Wordsworth and his sister Dorothy were living near Coleridge. The two poets believed that poetry should try to make the supernatural seem natural, and the natural, supernatural.

The carrying out of his idea produced a manuscript that was given to a London publisher in 1798. The *Lyrical **Ballads*** was brought out while Wordsworth and Coleridge were in Germany. The first edition met with unfavorable criticism. An enlarged edition with the famous *Preface by Wordsworth* was published in 1800; a third edition was published in 1802, a fourth in 1805. (With regard to procedure in this study, the poem "Tintern Abbey" is not included in the first chapter, although it did appear in the first edition of the *Lyrical Ballads*. The reason for this procedure is that the poem is simply not a "lyrical ballad." It will be studied in Chapter Three.)

SUBJECT MATTER AND AIMS OF WORDSWORTH'S POETRY

In the "Preface to the *Lyrical Ballads*" (1800), Wordsworth tells us that his poems were published as an experiment. He speaks about his poetic enterprise in this way because he is aware that he is not trying to cater to the public taste or to conform to established, traditional standards of what poetry is or should be.

Wordsworth in the "Preface" is in a sense warning the reader that the poems in the *Lyrical **Ballads*** might very well frustrate any expectations that the reader has for the customary kind of decorative poetry. One may summarize Wordsworth's ideas in "The Preface" in his way: Wordsworth (1) will write his poems about incidents and situations from common life, (2) will try to transform these incidents and situations by his imagination and present them in such a way that they will seem novel and "wonderful." (3) will try to trace through these humble incidents the essence of humanity, (4) will try to compose the poems in the kind of language that comes naturally to persons in normal conversation. Because of all these objectives, Wordsworth chose humble and rustic life. Men in the countryside live in close contact with nature and lead a simple life. The primary laws of humanity can be traced through their uncluttered, uncomplicated, uncorrupted lives. Moreover the language they use is plain and simple. There is throughout Wordsworth's work and throughout Romanticism as a literary movement the idea that God made the country and man made the city; the somewhat natural consequence is that people often think that God dwells in the country, and that evil dwells in the city.

HIS VALUES

Wordsworth is obviously trying to advocate simplicity and sincerity of thought and language as values essential to good poetry. Yet in his enthusiasm for these values he goes to the extreme of stating that the best language to be adopted by the poet is that which is really spoken by men. Wordsworth's own poetic practice sometimes contradicts his critical theories. The language of poetry is, and has always been, different from the language ordinarily used by men. But, many literary movements and innovations have claimed that they are making a return to the language really spoken by men. In defense of Wordsworth, however, it should be said that he quite probably meant not the actual words used in informal conversation but, rather, the idiom or rhythms of the spoken language. The reason for Wordsworth's being called "the Poet of the Democratic Idea" is in great measure evident in the "Preface," what with his stress on the great importance of humble personages and situations.

MORAL PURPOSE

Wordsworth affirms in the "Preface" that every poem of his has a moral or a purpose. But the moral of the poem, he carefully makes clear, should not be arbitrarily added to the poem. The moral that exists in a poem should be the inevitable conclusion of the poem itself. For Wordsworth, poetry is the outcome of the strong emotions of the poet. The poet (and also the reader) should train and regulate feelings by deep and long thinking, to such a degree that these feelings will be connected with important subjects.

Wordsworth states in the "Preface" that the actions and situations - that is to say, subject matter-in his poems are not important in themselves. It is the poet's feeling for this subject matter that gives the subject matter significance and endows it with a certain measure of importance. By feeling, Wordsworth certainly does not mean a mere formless expression of one's personal responses. It is a highly developed and sophisticated response that undergoes a rigorous intellectual discipline.

DIDACTICISM

It is obvious that Wordsworth considers himself a **didactic** poet, that is, a poet who tries to inculcate ethics through the medium of poetry. But he qualifies, the meaning of this also by differentiating himself from the 18th-century **didactic** poets; his poetic method differs from theirs when he says the moral should be an organic part of the poem. Wordsworth believes that the human mind is highly sensitive and discriminating. His own poetry, as he sees it, is an attempt to sharpen man's sensitivity even further, or at least to keep man's mind from any further blunting. Wordsworth considers that he is rendering society an excellent service, for there are in an industrialized society forces that conspire against man's natural sensitivity. For example, (1) the growing density of population in industrial areas vulgarizes taste and causes people to crave the extraordinary, and (2) the literature that caters to this appetite grinds off the discriminating edges of man's natural faculties. With regard to his vocation as a **didactic** poet, Wordsworth joined with his deep humanitarianism a highly developed historical sense. He tried with a nearly religious zeal to evolve an all-embracing poetics, one that could be of real relevance to man in industrial society.

WORDSWORTH'S POETIC STYLE

In his "Preface to the *Lyrical Ballads*," Wordsworth tells his reader that his poetry will be free of personifications because they do not occur in the language really used by men. Wordsworth is obviously reacting against the florid, overly-decorated style of late 18th-century poetry. Poets and critics had followed the belief that some words or expressions were more poetic than others. For instance, to write "denizens of the deep" was considered a more poetic usage than just fish, "the feathery tribe" more poetic than just birds. Wordsworth is trying to replace this consciously poetic language, this artificial **diction**, with the law of taste. His poetic faith affirms that no word is more poetical than any other word; it is only the context that should be the poet's prime concern.

WORDSWORTH'S CONCEPT OF THE VOCATION OF THE POET

The Wordsworthian poet is a man speaking to men: yet, he is more sensitive than other men, and his soul is more comprehensive and joyful. Moreover, his imaginative capacities are higher than those of the ordinary man. The principal function of the poet is to pierce through the surfaces of things in order to get at their essence. The universal truths he grasps should not be communicated through intellectual reasoning but, rather, should be "carried alive into the heart by passion." Nothing should stand as barrier between the poet and the nature that surrounds him.

HIS DEMOCRACY

Wordsworth is trying to reconcile, and with considerable success, his democratic ideal of equality with his belief in the uniqueness of the individual human being - particularly of the poet. We should be especially mindful of the way in which Wordsworth stresses that the poet is like the rest of men, yet different, different not in quality but only in degree. We should note especially also Wordsworth's emphasis on the importance of the immediate confrontation between the poet and things. Wordsworth's poetry is the outcome of the exchange between the mind of the poet and nature.

Wordsworth believes that the mind of man is exquisitely fitted to the universe, and that a relationship of mutual exchange should exist between them. "He [the Poet] considers man and nature as essentially adapted to each other, and the mind of man as naturally the mirror of the fairest and most interesting properties of nature."

WORDSWORTH AND SCIENCE

Wordsworth does not reject the possibility of making science and its findings the subject matter of his poetry. Poetry for him is the most comprehensive expression of man's totality and achievements. Because of the comprehensiveness of poetry, the poet should not **refrain** from going side by side with the man of science. The poet is the emissary of all truth to man; through bringing truth to man, he helps to bind the human community together in "relationship and love."

WORDSWORTH'S IDEAS ABOUT POETIC METER

Towards the end of the "Preface" Wordsworth gives what he considers to be a necessary defense of his use of poetic meter in the poems published in the *Lyrical Ballads*. Whereas poetic **diction** (the choice of language, particularly in the sense of figurative language) is "arbitrary, and subject to infinite caprices upon which no calculation whatever can be made," poetic meter "is regular and uniform. . . ." Wordsworth thinks of poetic **diction** as putting the reader at the mercy of the poet, whereas he considers that both poet and reader submit to meter. In a sense, poetic **diction** is not democratic, whereas poetic meter is. A second reason for writing in meter, says Wordsworth, is that meter acts as a regularizing, coordinating agent in poems, in poems that might otherwise tend toward being a liquid, formless mass of emotion. Wordsworth makes reference to the old **ballads** in support of this position on the use of poetic meter.

A third reason that Wordsworth gives for using poetic meter is what he calls the "principle [that] is the great spring of the activity of our minds, and their chief feeder." This is the principle of the perception of similitude in dissimilitude. Wordsworth considers this principle to be at the very basis of our processes of thought and feeling.

Wordsworth considers that meter is actually at work in human behavior, both with regard to one's intellectual concepts, and courses of action that come from following these intellectual concepts. Meter is a principle of the similar that acts to unify the dissimilar.

Finally, because the poet writes about real things, he runs the risk that his reader might be overpowered by the reality that is the poet's subject matter. If the poem overpowers the reader and confuses him, it is of course a failure. The poem is a failure because the reader fails at being able to read the poetic composition as an organic unity. The "music of harmonious metrical language," says Wordsworth, is one of the principles "which is of the most important use in tempering the painful feeling always found intermingled with powerful descriptions of the deeper passions."

Meter serves to create a certain distance that keeps art distinct from reality.

Wordsworth had spoken before in the "Preface" of meter as a "super-added pleasure." In later paragraphs he seems to take a more definite position in considering meter as an essential, not simply an extra element in poetic composition.

WORDSWORTH'S FAMOUS DEFINITION OF POETRY

We will do well in studying Wordsworth to take careful cognizance of his emphasis on "emotion recollected in tranquillity." He is being very cautious in his definition to disqualify mere emotion as fit subject matter for poetry. The "mood" in which poetry is written is not just emotion but contemplated emotion. One may be accurate in calling this regularizing and purifying faculty of the poet's mind his memory, but we should be careful to think of this faculty as having powers more highly complex and sophisticated than those we attach to the memory, as we normally use that term. It is not just remembrance that Wordsworth is talking about, but, rather, a separation of the elements of reality, a maturing contemplation of them in their separateness and uniqueness, and then a reunion of them, a modifying blending of them into a higher and more meaningful unity, which could not have been true of them in their original state as raw materials. In this regard, Wordsworth's concept of the function of the poetic imagination would be similar to that of Samuel Taylor Coleridge, who contributed important influence and direction for Wordsworth in his composition of the "Preface." Coleridge considered the imagination to be the active, assertive power in man (particularly in the man of poetic imagination) that goes forth into the surrounding natural order and gives it a form, shape, and unity that it could not in its natural state possess. Memory is not, therefore, to be considered a passive faculty, but, rather, an active one.

CENTRAL IDEAS

The "Preface" is an important document. It should occupy a central place in the attention of the student of Wordsworth's poetry. Such ideas as the adaptation of the mind of man to nature, and the interest in humble persons and humble situations have an abiding importance in a reading of Wordsworth. The "Preface" contains some of Wordsworth's best comments on his own poetry and his own method of poetic creation. It seems characteristic of his poetry that composition is not a spur-of-the-moment matter, but, to the contrary, is an act of emotion recollected in tranquility. Any reading of the "Preface," nevertheless, should be a critical reading. The student should be aware of certain departures from principles in actual poetic practice. Particularly with respect to the matter of the best language for poetry, the reader of Wordsworth should ask if the poems speak in "a selection of language really used by men."

THE MAJOR POETRY

THE REVERIE OF POOR SUSAN

Wordsworth says that the idea of the poem was suggested to him by the "affecting" singing of birds in the streets of London "during the freshness and stillness of the Spring morning." Poor Susan, and emigrant from the countryside, passes daily by a spot where a thrush has sung loudly at daylight for a period of three years. She is completely enchanted with the song of the bird; her imagination is stirred, so stirred that she has a vision of a mountain, trees, "volumes of vapour," and a flowing river. She sees the green pastures where she used to walk and the cottage she lived in while she was still in the country. But as she looks, in the midst of her visionary exaltation, the scenes pass away from her sight; she cannot any longer see what she had seen.

Comment

There is an obvious opposition established in this poem between the life in the country and the life in the city. All of the blessed sights and sounds in nature that are so easily found and rejoiced in the countryside can only be discovered in the city through an act of creative imagination. The setting and character of the village is that of openness and freedom, and these qualities give one a sense of belonging, a sense of rootedness, a sense of security. Such gifts are not to be discovered in the city. Wordsworth's image of the flowing river serves his poetic purpose in conveying to the reader the feeling of space and movement.

THE MAJOR POETRY

WE ARE SEVEN

Wordsworth says this poem is based on an actual conversation that he had with a little girl whom he met within the area of Goodrich Castle in the year 1793. Wordsworth tells us that the meeting occurred as he journeyed to North Wales where he spent the summer of 1793 with the father of his friend, Robert Jones. In the introduction of "We Are Seven" he relates further that this poem was composed specifically for publication in the *Lyrical Ballads,* the plan of which was conceived by Wordsworth and Coleridge in the spring of 1798.

The simple child in the poem, full of energy and that joy in life that has not yet been invaded by an adult awareness of the grim facts of sorrow, separation, and death, knows really nothing about the blackness in the heart of mortal things. The child still without a consciousness of time and history has not come under the heavy weight of the limits of mortality. Wordsworth opens the poem with a rhetorical question of four lines designed to state this fact:

_____ A Simple child, That lightly draws its breath, And feels its life in every limb, What should it know of death?

The whole poem is an illustration of the message of this stanza. The poet met this eight-year-old cottage girl whose beauty gladdened his heart. He asked her how many sisters and brothers she had, and she answered him "seven." But upon further questioning of her, the poet discovered that the little girl's sister, Jane, and her brother, John, were both dead; yet she insisted on counting them among the living. The poet, bound by the heavy chains of time-consciousness, tried to convince the little girl that her sisters and brothers really numbered only five since two had already died. But, she, with no real consciousness of the meaning of death, does not feel the impact of the separation; she visits Jane and John daily at their graves, she knits her stockings there, she hems her kerchief, she eats her supper at their side. The poet found that he was throwing words away in his own adult mathematical calculations of her family. She does not have to see - she is indeed unable to see - the world through the smudged glasses of mortal consciousness. She still lives in close harmony with the great spirit of life that moves through all things. The poet says "But they are dead; those two are dead! "But the little girl answers with passionate firmness, "Nay, we are seven!"

Comment

Most simply, the poem is about the inability of children to conceive of the notion of death. But the Wordsworthian profundity goes much deeper than this. The poem is also a contemplation of, an examination of the wretched limits that cut the adult off from the wellsprings of divine security and joy, from which the "Simple child" constantly draws meaning, purpose, perhaps even the assurance of eternal Providence. "We Are Seven" must nearly necessarily be read as a poem of

metaphysical rebellion. It is the awareness of the existence of death that differentiates the mature man from the simple child. It is not a differentiation that the poet in "We Are Seven" accepts gracefully. He objects loudly to the expulsion from Eden. This objection makes up a recurrent theme in Wordsworth's poetry; perhaps its most famous treatment is in the "Ode: Intimations of Immortality from Recollections of Early Childhood." The state of childhood is a blessing that one does not easily learn to live without. The replacement of it with the adult responsibility of making complex decisions and reaping their all-too-frequent bitter fruit is a sorry second-best. One may feel the Biblical longing for unbroken fellowship with the Father as an inevitable level of hope in the poet's envious and despairing remonstrance in "We Are Seven." He may ardently correct the little girl, and say to her something like, "Come on, grow up," but she is yet free of the consciousness that plagues him. We may say in this respect that "We Are Seven" is a two-level poem in the manner of "A Slumber Did My Spirit Seal" and "Surprised by Joy - Impatient as the Wind." Two sharply contradictory levels of understanding of the same problem vibrate against each other, yet each level has an inherent value of its own, and its own integral right to exist.

THE MAJOR POETRY

THE THORN

It would seem that the subject of the poem is the Thorn that the poet, or, more accurately, that the narrator had seen - the old, grey, wretched, forlorn thing that stands erect like a stone. But the subject is really Martha Ray and her misery. The Thorn becomes a kind of **metaphor** for the woman who had been courted by Stephen Hill and then abandoned by him after she became pregnant with his child

The natural setting in the poem is the Thorn, located less than five yards from the mountain path that goes

High on a mountain's highest ridge, Where oft the stormy winter gale Cuts like a scythe, while through the clouds It sweeps from vale to vale....

Only three yards from the Thorn there is a small pond of muddy water. Strangely, although it is "bare / To thirsty suns and parching air," it is never dried. Beneath the Thorn there is a mound of multi-colored moss. In fact, the beautiful colors of the mound are one of its most remarkable features; the other, of course, is the miraculous movement it once made when some of the towns - people tried to dig it up. But the narrator is especially careful to describe the beautiful colors of the mound:

All lovely colours there you see, All colours that were ever seen; And mossy network too is there, As if by hand of lady fair The work had woven been; And cups, the darlings of the eye, So deep is their vermilion dye.

Ah me! what lovely tints are there Of olive green and scarlet bright, In spikes, in branches, and in stars, Green, red, and pearly white!

The first introduction that is made of the story of Martha Ray comes in the description that the narrator is giving of the mound. He compares the mound in size to an infant's grave.

The introduction of Martha Ray comes after the description that the narrator gives of the mountain area surrounding the Thorn. He makes the transition from the scene to the person by advising that if any be interested in seeing this leaveless, briarless Thorn, this colorful mound, this gale-driven, cloud-swept region, he should go there at a carefully selected time, a time when Martha Ray is in her hut; the narrator tells that he "never heard of such as dare / Approach the spot when she is there." Martha Ray goes to this place at all times, both in the day and in the night, and in all kinds of weather. She wears a scarlet cloak and cries to herself in the words, "Oh misery! oh misery! / Oh woe is me! oh misery!" She has a special relationship to the natural forces that surround her: "And she is known to every star, / And every wind that blows . . . ." In this regard she bears a definite similarity to what Wordsworth would consider the poet to be. No one really knows, the narrator says, why Martha Ray goes to the place of the mound beneath the Thorn. But he proceeds from this point to tell the tragic story of her life, of "her who sate / In misery near the miserable Thorn," as Wordsworth summarizes in *The Prelude* the subject of the mariner's narration.

Martha Ray was deserted by Stephen Hill, her lover, some twenty-two years before. She had been in her relationship with him "blithe and gay," she had with "true good-will" given "Her company to Stephen Hill," and her friends and her kinfolk had looked with approval on her choice. Martha Ray and Stephen Hill set a date for their marriage, but Stephen proved to be a person of infidelity and treachery, for he had already made promises to another woman, and "with this other Maid" he pledged marriage vows. Stephen's careless disregard of Martha's welfare brought her dismay and sorrow. It was apparently her first experience with human degeneracy. She did not have the brutality of former confrontations to strengthen her resources: "A fire was kindled in her breast, / Which might not burn itself to rest." There is a change in the narration at this point in the poem (line 122). What the narrator has told so far is intended to be taken as fact: he begins the next chapter of his story with "They say," and apparently we are to season somehow the following events with at least a grain of the salt of doubt. But, then, in another sense, the possibility that what follows is not absolute chronological fact might serve poetically to strengthen our faith in its truth. The mariner's story in its very strangeness might prove to be much more effective than newspaper history in creating "that willing suspension of disbelief for the moment, which constitutes poetic faith." However much we may proclaim our doubt in the supernatural, we all somewhere yearn to believe it. From the "They say" of line 122, the narrator relates that six months after Stephen had deserted Martha she was big with child, a child that is now presumed to be buried under the mound of earth over which the Thorn grows. There are some people who tell that Martha hanged her baby on the tree, some tell that she drowned the baby in the pond, some say that the moss is red because of the color of the baby's blood. There are some people who testify that they have observed the shadow of the baby in the pond, and that anyone who goes there and fixes a steady eye on the water can see it. Some have even said that they have heard voices of the living and the dead coming from the direction of the mountain. Once when the more judicious element of the population sought to find evidence of the woman's crime against her child, they found that the hill of moss moved miraculously before their eyes and that the grass upon the ground shook. Although the people could not recover the infant's bones in order to have sufficient proof for bringing the woman to public justice, they still think that the mound contains Martha Ray's child by Stephen Hill.

Comment

The poem is in a sense framed by the existence and the character of the Thorn. The first two **stanzas** and the last one are concerned with this "wretched thing forlorn." There is more than just the measurement of its size in the poet's **metaphor** of the "two years' child" in the opening **stanza**. In one way and another, the Thorn becomes in the progress of the poem emblematic of the story the mariner tells.

From the way in which the narrator talks about the people of the town, the Thorn is a representation of crimes, crimes that can include child-murder. There is probably an intended association between the way in which the Thorn struggles for life in the midst of the raw forces of nature, at one and the same time beautiful and fierce, and the way Martha Ray must struggle to preserve her own tenuous grasp on the strength of life in the midst of the raw forces of human unkindness and disregard. Stephen Hill's insensitivity is in a way continued by the villagers;

they do not comprehend, either, the meaning of Martha Ray's suffering: they are not as sympathetic, genuinely sympathetic, as they are merely curious.

FORM

At line 78 in the poem it becomes evident that Wordsworth is using dialogue. He has adapted a standard technique in traditional **ballads** to his own poetic purposes - and adapted it well. It is one of his most frequently-used devices in the short poems of the years 1797 to 1802. It is central in such poems, different as they are, as "We Are Seven," "The Idiot Boy," "The Fountain," "Expostulation and Reply," and "Michael" even.

CHARACTER

Martha Ray can probably be numbered among Wordsworth's "solitaries." Failing to find human sympathy, or, perhaps, better, mutually meaningful human relationships, she withdrew from the human community and became "known to every star, / And to every wind that blows...." In a sense her life becomes more meaningful for her withdrawal. This is not so strange; it is after all a poem written by a poet who did very nearly the same thing. It should be clarified, though, that withdrawal is with the "solitaries" not always merely the measure of their own independent decision; they are in a measure the objects of cosmic forces that come to bear on them. Martha Ray's solitariness is sometimes discussed in the terms of the "deserted mother" motif, which is quite recurrent in Wordsworth's poetry. The British critic, Sir Herbert Read, attributes this **theme** to the poet's own sense of guilt over having left Annette Vallon, the woman he fell in love with in Orleans, during his stay in France in 1792, and who bore him a daughter. There is probably no discounting the influence of this event in Wordsworth's life. There should also be introduced the fact, however, that it was conventional for **ballads** to have at Wordsworth's time deserted mothers as subject matter.

"The Thorn" is a good poem for the study of Wordsworth's experimentation with language. It is one of the poems in which his ultimately impractical ideal of using "the real language of men" comes close to realization.

THE MAJOR POETRY

SIMON LEE

The full title of this poem is "Simon Lee The Old Huntsman; with an Incident in which He Was Concerned," In this poem, as in most of the poems of the *Lyrical Ballads,* Wordsworth takes an incident to which he has been witness or in which he has participated, or one that has come to him from some other witness or participant. Here the poet has had an actual encounter with The Old Huntsman.

This poem is a good example of Wordsworth's ambitions as a poet to make a return to the primitive, pristine state of English poetry that existed when English letters were what he considered they should be.

Old Simon Lee lives "In the sweet shire of Cardigan, / Not far from pleasant Ivor-hall. . . ." It is said that this now diminutive old man was once strong and vital. He ran as a merry huntsman for a full thirty-five years; "still the centre of his cheek / Is red as a ripe cherry." In his vital days there was no one who could rival him in the blowing of the hunting horn and in the keeping of the pace of the hunt.

He all the country could outrun, Could leave both man and horse behind; And often, ere the chase was done, He reeled, and was stone-blind.

But now Simon's health had faded, and his former feudal master has died. He is now shrunken in body to only a shadow of what he once was; "thin and dry" legs reach down to swollen and thick ankles. He is now in his old age "bereft / Of health, strength, friends, and kindred. . . ." He is victimized by poverty, and all he can claim of the past riches of his relationships and active life is the companionship of his wife.

One prop he has, and only one, His wife, an aged woman, Lives with him, near the waterfall, Upon the village Common.

The only material possessions to which they lay claim are a "scrap of land" and "their moss-grown hut of clay. . . ." Simon can look forward to nothing but continually failing health and only a few months of life.

Few months of life has he in store As he to you will tell, For still, the more he works, the more Do his weak ankles swell.

At this point the poet breaks off his description of Simon's condition in his old age and addresses himself to the reader. He anticipates that the reader expects a story out of all of this. But tale there is none, except that the reader might be poet enough himself to find "A tale in everything."

O Reader had you in your mind Such stories as silent thought can bring, O gentle Reader! you would find A tale in everything. What more I have to say is short, And you must kindly take it: It is no tale; but, should you think, Perhaps a tale you'll make it.

But it is evident also that if the reader will see what the poet sees, he must be what the poet is - first of all a philosopher. The **stanza** is very nearly a statement of part of Wordsworth's poetic credo:

What is a Poet? He is a man speaking to men: a man, it is true, endowed with more lively sensibility, more enthusiasm and tenderness, who has a greater knowledge of human nature, and a more comprehensive soul, than are supposed to be common among mankind To these qualities he has added a disposition to be affected more than other men by absent things as if they were present The Poet is chiefly distinguished from other men by a greater promptness to think and feel without immediate external excitement

The poet in "Simon Lee" says he has no tale to relate to the reader, but it is an account of an event, a meeting between the poet and old Simon Lee. While passing by Simon on a summer-day, the poet finds the old man trying to dig a root out of the ground with a mattock. But because of the weakness he has come to suffer in his old age, Simon might have gone on digging forever at the stump without moving it. The poet tells that

The mattock tottered in his hand; So vain was his endeavour, That at the root of the old tree He might have worked for ever.

The poet asks Simon if he might offer him help in the task, and Simon accepts. The poet takes the mattock in hand, and with a single blow he severs the tangled root with which Simon had been so long struggling. Simon is so deeply moved by the poet's generosity that it seems he will never stop thanking him. The poem ends as the poet contemplates the experience with generosity that has come out of his meeting with The Old Huntsman.

- I've heard of hearts unkind, kind deeds With coldness still returning; Alas! the gratitude of men Hath oftener left me mourning.

Comment

We may very well find in this poem a current of revolt against the perfectionist philosophy of the eighteenth century. That philosophy would not find room within its cold rationalism for such a humble (however profound) emotion as gratitude. There is a childlike quality in the thanksgiving that the old huntsman expresses to the poet. Obviously gratitude is not an emotion that one comes to acquire because one acquires either wealth or power. The poem is obviously not about Simon's Master who lived in the Hall of Ivor, and Simon in his prime cared about more important things than "husbandry or tillage." "To blither tasks did Simon rouse / The sleepers of the village." Gratitude is a human gift that lies far beneath any one or thousand "things" that one might collect. It is a capacity that is at the heart of what is naturally human and humane. The poem is obviously about a subject drawn from "humble and rustic life." A more heroic subject would have been some incident in the life of Simon at the Hall of Ivor. As literature, "Simon Lee" shows the Wordsworthian reaction against the conventional 18th-century tales of knights and ladies and chivalric adventure, just as Wordsworth's poem "Michael" is for one thing a conspicuous contrast to the aristocratic pastorals that are filled with shepherds and shepherdesses. The life of Simon Lee as subject matter for the poem is as close to the earth as the stubborn stump at which he has vainly hacked.

THE MAJOR POETRY

LINES WRITTEN IN EARLY SPRING

There is a great deal of geographical particularity in Wordsworth's poems. He may be talking about nature in a whole, inclusive sense, but the focus of a particular poem is usually a pinpoint on the planet Earth. There is something obviously deliberate here. It is as if Wordsworth as a nature poet knew nature meaningfully only because he had proceeded to the general by way of the carefully observed particular. This may seem an unnecessary statement of the obvious, but most student discussions of "nature" poets are too loose to be accurate. The reader of Wordsworth should be careful to observe the deliberate way the poet anchors a poem, or the experience a poem is about, in a particular scene.

"Lines Written in Early Spring" belongs naturally to a group of four poems in *Lyrical Ballads*. The other three, "To My Sister," "Expostulation and Reply," and "The Tables Turned," share with the poem here under consideration an obvious simplicity of **diction**, a directness of address, a didacticism in purpose. Wordsworth was later to call all of them "Poems of Sentiment and Reflection." The simplicity of approach is not, however, naive. The poems may approach at times a quality of the childlike, but they never touch the border of the childish; these words, of course, mean very different things.

The poet says in "Lines Written in Early Spring" that he had while sitting in a grove heard the songs of many birds. His mood was one "when pleasant thoughts / Bring sad thoughts to the mind." He sees all around him the "fair works" of Nature. In fact, Nature is so much alive that he finds natural objects in possession of human senses: "And 'tis my faith that every flower / Enjoys the air it breathes." The degree of animation in Nature extends so far that she acts as a force to link him to what he sees and hears: "To her fair works did Nature link / The human soul that through me ran. . . ." The marriage between the poet and Nature is so great that there is no boundary any more between thought and feeling. The degree of sympathetic identification is of such a measure that the motion of the birds becomes a thrill within his own nervous system.

The only jarring note in the whole symphony is "What man has made of man." It is this awareness that introduces tautness into the poet's otherwise passive state. The second and the last **stanzas** contain the dissonance of the shock of recognition: the human evil of waste of what is divinely human.

Comment

The poem may be said to be based on a simple, though infinitely correct, contrast between man and nature. But Wordworth's relationship to nature is usually more complex than what we have in "Lines Written in Early Spring." Perhaps the simple contrast is deliberate here because Wordsworth at the time was still in the process of inaugurating new attitudes in poetry, diligently trying to change the tastes of his readers.

This is one of a body of Wordsworth's poems, sometimes called "doctrinal poems." (See above for three other examples of the type.) One may rightly enumerate at least four characteristics that they have in common: (1) the simplicity of rhetoric is consciously, carefully designed; (2) there is usually the presence of bare precepts, often through the implementation of contrast; (3) there is running through all of them the **theme** of "wise passiveness"; (4) the didacticism is not from a teacher who is in any way trying to hide the fact that he is a teacher. Perhaps we can say that Wordsworth's device was consciously to neglect part of the truth in order to make some point forcefully. In this sense these poems have the character of a manifesto.

We are easily reminded of Wordsworth's statements in the "Preface" about the relationship between nature and the human mind when we read such lines as,

To her fair works did Nature link The human soul that through me ran; The birds around me hopped and played, Their thoughts I cannot measure: - But the least motion which they made, It seemed a thrill of pleasure.

It is not unfair to take this poem and other poems of this group as useful sources of Wordsworth's ideas, but for a more rightly comprehensive understanding, the reader should go to the later (and more mature) poems and look closely for differences. The unalloyed joyfulness, the antithetical contrasts, the aphoristic statements become merged in Wordsworth's later poems into more complex and subtle articulations. For this kind of productive comparative reading, one might go immediately from a reading of "Lines Written in Early Spring" to "Tintern Abbey."

THE MAJOR POETRY

TO MY SISTER

This poem and the two following say to leave barren books behind and come forth into a fresh confrontation with natural forces. "To My Sister" has a specific message, directly stated. Again the language is plain talk; the poet makes no effort to be witty. There are no **metaphysical** conceits here, no consciously poetic inventiveness. The open kind of declaration that Wordsworth is using would become all the more vivid with, say, John Donne's devilish kind of cleverness as a background. No convoluted compass **metaphors** here - just,

Love, now a universal birth, From heart to heart is stealing, From earth to man, from man to earth: - It is the hour of feeling.

The form of address in the poem is the poet speaking to his sister, just as the plain title tells. He is saying to her that in the first day of March there is universal joy. The harbinger of the resurgence of life is the robin; he has come like the dove that returned to Noah, but his perching place is nothing so elaborate as an ark, only the sturdy wood of the larch tree that grows near the poet's door. The things of nature have both silent and noisy communion with each other. The air, for example, brings a blessing to trees, and mountains (both bare from the season passing), and to the grass. The poet asks his sister to come with him from the breakfast table into the open stretches of the out-of-doors. It is a wish of his, he says, "Come forth and feel the sun." Her attire for the occasion should be in harmony with the simple currents of joy that pulsate along the interconnected network of nature's being and the poet's being: "Put on with speed your woodland dress. . . ." All connections with the sophistications of civilization should be cut on such a day - no books; no ponderous contemplation of social, political, institutional problems; no "joyless forms" of botanical analysis nor organized directions to the picturesque (William Gilpin); no presuppositions to be carefully rational. The poet says to his sister that this new day of life in resurgence can only rightly be celebrated with a primitive in-touchness with the elements that have rolled and thinned and flowed from the first blaze and splash of creation. ". . . for this one day / We'll give to idleness. / . . . . / It is the hour of feeling." In such a time it may be that one moment will store up treasures within, that book-stooping, squinting, brow-furrowing labor could never provide. The impressions left within the deep layers of the mind by what they drink in this day will guide them in future days. And so, a key **stanza** in the poem is,

Some silent laws our heart will make, Which they shall long obey: We for the year to come may take Our temper from to-day.

Comment

This is another poem in the general flow of composition of "Expostulation and Reply" and "The Tables Turned," both with regard to **diction**, direction, and doctrine. Wordsworth advocates "wise passiveness." His appeal to sister Dorothy is not mere escape to leafy nooks. We miss the point - we miss even the whole target - if we think that the poet means something less than absolutely serious reorientation. The terms of the invitation may be jocund, as the experience will be, but it is the jovial, the glad, the delightful within a context of utterly serious purpose; the purpose is on a par with something like conversion to Christ! The passiveness the poet proffers is not so much cognitive as osmotic. The three persons mentioned in the poem will fix themselves to the flow of new life. The poetic language in which the day's excursion is couched is therefore sensuous. The love the poet associates with the season is not conceived in the higher floors of the cerebrum: this is not intellectual, platonic, fraternal, or familial love - this is love that tingles along nerve fibers, that seeps in through pores. One does not contemplate the sights and sounds of this day as a witness to Divine Providence. Divine spirit may be there, but as "the blessed power that rolls / About, below, above. . . ." It is consequently safe to say that Wordsworth's so-called paganism has reached an extreme in this poem, at least if one measures paganism by the standards of orthodox theology. Wordsworth is little concerned with the historically-centered proclamations of the Christian Faith. In fact, he suggests a new kind of calendar, one with the B.C. and A.D. removed. The birth of Christ as a dating device will be replaced by what is happening in each of the sweet minutes of this "first mild day of March." If there must be historical consciousness - though within the feeling of this poem such a thing is irrelevant - let it be determined only by the creature's feeling of the new season, not by the dull historical claims of a far-off desert people.

THE MAJOR POETRY

EXPOSTULATION AND REPLY

Wordsworth's explanatory note on this poem helps to clarify the setting. He tells that "Expostulation and Reply" and the companion poem "The Tables Turned" both "arose out of conversation with a friend [William Hazlitt] who was somewhat unreasonably attached to modern books of moral philosophy." The speeches in the poem are from the author (the same openness about the author's identity is present in this poem) and from "his good friend Matthew." The author has his own name, William; Matthew is Hazlitt.

The first three **stanzas** contain Matthew's remonstrance; the last four **stanzas** contain William's reply. Matthew is astonished at the poet's idleness and dreaminess:

'Why, William, on that old grey stone, Thus for the length of half a day, Why, William, sit you thus alone, And dream your time away?'

The charge that Matthew levels at William is that the poet is neglecting books, those sources of light (reason) that past generations pass as flaming torches across the centuries. He admonishes him, "Up! up! and drink the spirit breathed / From dead men to their kind." He considers William's state to be simply idleness: he considers that the poet has forgotten his own obligation to his fellow human kind, both to his present society and to the men who will follow him in future times. The purpose of human life must, Matthew says, have an obvious thrust of energy toward definite moral objectives. In such a passive state as the Poet's, there is no concrete accomplishment. In one **stanza** of his objection to William's "indolence," Matthew makes an introduction to what the poet will say in reply, to what the poet will affirm as the real truth of his present relations to what is around him. Matthew says to him,

'You look round on your Mother Earth, As if she for no purpose bore you; As if you were her first-born birth, And none had lived before you!'

It is just such a primitive relationship to "Mother Earth" that is the source of greater wisdom. Matthew advises the poet to return to the intellectual pursuit of moral philosophy in order to understand his place in the scheme of things and what that place demands of him in way of obligation to humankind. But the message of the poem, introduced by the transitional **stanza** locating the conversation at Esthwaite lake, is that one learns just what Matthew is advising William to learn, but through the mysterious ebb and flow of "Powers" in the universe "Which of themselves our mind impress. . . ." The means of receiving them is not busy turning of pages, but "wise passiveness." The most exact thing that William says in the poem about the way it all happens is in **stanza** five:

'The eye-it cannot choose but see; We cannot bid the ear be still; Our bodies feel, where'er they be, Against or with our will.'

In short, truth comes to us in important means that we cannot discover through seeking; to go scrambling after it would be to break the limbs off the tree before the fruit has ripened.

Comment

This is another interesting poem to read for what it reveals about the relationship of the mind of man to the universe in which he lives. But, again, for the larger dimensions of the subject, one must read other poems that Wordsworth wrote. For example, in a poem of about four years later, "Near Dover," the statement is, "Winds blow, and waters roll, / Strength to the brave, and Power, and Deity; / Yet in themselves are nothing!" To choose a more famous example, and one from a poem closer in chronology to "Expostulation and Reply," there are the lines in "Tintern Abbey" that comment on the process of the poet's encounter with "all that we behold / From this green earth . . .," although the lines are not entirely contradictory to the definition of process in the **stanza** beginning "'The eye - it cannot choose but see'. . . ." After reviewing at length the history of his life among nature's "beauteous forms," Wordsworth affirmed about human perception: ". . . of all the mighty world / Of eye, and ear, - both what they half create, / And what perceive. . . ." It is essentially a question of saying either that nature is all, and we have only to submit ourselves to her many forms and aspects to realize ourselves fully, or that the power of the human mind - usually termed imagination - must go forth into nature and animate and shape her furnishings into a meaningful, unified whole. The issue is central in Coleridge's "Dejection: An Ode." Probably Wordsworth really wanted to have it both ways - Coleridge also. The impossible ideal was to have nature as the source of man's true understanding of his purposes, and of the poet's inspiration, and yet maintain that the mind of man is the highest concentration of creative energy and inspiration in the universe. It is likely the more representative Wordsworthian attitude, considering all his poems at once, that the relationship between nature and the mind of man is one of "ennobling interchange." The mind, or the imagination, receives, but must also give.

"Expostulation and Reply" is one of Wordsworth's most anti-intellectual poems. But, this is not any final statement of idea. Wordsworth always had profound respect for human learning. One productive line of interpretation is to read the poem as a violent reaction against eighteenth-century narrow-minded rationalism, against the elevation of the human reason into a place of supremacy in human values.

THE MAJOR POETRY

THE TABLES TURNED

The subtitle identifies this poem as an intended sequel to "Expostulation and Reply": "An Evening Scene on the Same Subject." This poem is probably most famous for the sixth stanza:

One impulse from a vernal wood May teach you more of man, Of moral evil and of good, Than all the sages can.

It is obviously another anti-book poem. "Books! 'tis dull and endless strife...." Not only do they create problems in posture, as the second line of the poem puts it in catchy simplicity, but worse, they cloud man's countenance.

The content here is further answer to the poet's admonisher in the former poem. The tables are turned in precisely the sense that now William has his chance to remonstrate his remonstrator. The first **stanza** even expresses a kind of surprise that Matthew (though that name is not used in this poem) puts himself under the weight of heavy print: "Why all this toil and trouble?" It is clearly not worth it! And exclamation points are in order, for they are used in the poem no less than eight times in the first thirteen lines. The poet obviously intends to be definite. He tells this book-worm friend to "Come forth into the light of things. . . ." As noted previously, this is really the call of all the poems in this doctrinal group.

Nature should be the teacher, not books. There is more wisdom in the song of the linnet, there is a finer sermon in the song of the throstle; the cold waters of bookish philosophy can give nothing of the joy that one finds in the flood of the sun's "freshening lustre mellow," "His first sweet evening yellow." In gnomic exactness Wordsworth names the sages and their cloistered dissertations on the nature of moral evil. But one does not learn about the essence of man's being and the substance of the problems that threaten it through myopic fixation on pages covered with ink by men who had myopic fixation on pages, and so on. William advises, receive the impulse from the vernal wood. With exactness he names also the disciplines of human learning that "murder to dissect." Man's "meddling intellect" does not order, but, rather, "Mis-shapes." One learns about things through the ministry of "the beauteous forms of things," and it is to them that Matthew - and all men, of course - should bring the open heart, the heart of "wise passiveness," the heart "That watches and receives." "Enough of Science and of Art. . . ."

Comment

One of the most conspicuous characteristics of this poem is its unobstructed spontaneity. The language of the first four **stanzas** works well to prepare the listener for the teaching in the last four stanzas. Spontaneous response in his listener is what the poet expects from the jolting entreaty he gives in the words, "Up! up! . . . / . . . Up! up!" Then he enriches the invitation by moving in spontaneous stream-of-consciousness style from the sun to the linnet to the throstle. The message of the last **stanza** is, fittingly, "Come forth," but do not come with presuppositions, with preconceived notions of what should be; rather, bring "a heart / That watches and receives" whatever may happen in one's privileged ken.

Wordsworth's reaction against any kind of narrow-minded, mechanical intellectualism is again at work in this poem, but one should not conclude that he was categorically opposed to the work or the findings of "Science and of Art." To be fair to the poem, and to the poet, one must read "The Tables Turned" (and the other poems we have been reading in this chapter) in the historical context that belongs to it. It is the desiccated rationalists' promotion of books to the neglect of an elemental contact with a dynamic universe that Wordsworth is striking out against. As Wordsworth's **sonnet** puts it, "The world is too much with us." There is the reaction also in language. Wordsworth felt that English poetry had become bogged down in the superficialities of eighteenth-century poetic **diction**; "The Tables Turned" has language that is so conversational that it is nearly prose.

THE LUCY POEMS

The Lucy Poems are five pieces, all of which are elegiac in character. They are usually studied as a unit, as the heading above suggests. They probably should be read as closely related, but for more reasons than the appearance in the poems of the name Lucy; the girl about whom the poems are written stands in a special kind of relationship to nature - this perhaps more than anything else makes a family of these poems. She is very nearly one with the moon, with "untrodden ways," with bowers and green fields, with "mute insensate things," "With rocks, and stones, and trees." The poems are alike also in their fundamental meter of the iambic foot, though there are also many variations.

They have, as suggested above, a generally meditative temper. One critic says that they have a prototype in the meditative verse of classical times. There may be indeed the meditation of Greek and Latin poems in the background, but there is no doubt also the various personality traits of the English folk **ballad**. The lament of these poems uses the lyrical heartbeat; the person loved is not concretized in the marble of human fame; rather, she is missed and yearned for in the warmth of human tears. Unlike the doctrinal pieces included in the *Lyrical Ballads,* there is in the *Lucy Poems* such established poetic usages as **similes** and metaphors. Lucy is described by Wordsworth as half-hidden like the violet, as solitary as the one star that shines in the sky. Most classroom lectures for undergraduates on the *Lucy Poems* at one time or another seem always to include reference to their "noble simplicity"; but, the matter needs more refinement than this. There is an easily spotted artistic use of understatement in these poems. The full impact of it can be felt in such lines as "But she is in her grave, and, oh, / The difference to me." The problem is what makes for "noble simplicity."

LUCY HERSELF

Who is the Lucy around whom all these poems are written? No one knows the answer to that question, but there are some good theories: (1) Lucy is an unknown maiden to whom the poet had pledged his love in his youth; (2) biographically, Lucy may have been Mary Hutchinson, the young woman who eventually became the poet's wife; (3) again biographically, Margaret Hutchinson, the sister of Mary, who had died in 1796; (4) more intimately biographical than Margaret Hutchinson, Lucy is Dorothy Wordsworth, the poet's sister, who brought the poet through one of the great crises of his life by sharpening his vision toward nature in a remarkably sensitive way; (5) Annette Vallon, the unmarried mother ("deserted mother") of Wordsworth's daughter, Caroline, (6) an unidentified Mary of the area of Esthwaite Water, about whom Wordsworth in his youth wrote several poems. It may be the safest bet of all to assume that Lucy is a composite figure of many, if not all, of these persons and influences. Finally, and less importantly, all these poems have the element of homesickness that characterized the stay that William and Dorothy Wordsworth had in Germany in the bitter Goslar winter of 1798. In this regard, Lucy may serve in all of these poems as a symbol for the many elements of English life for which the poet was yearning while away, while studying and walking in Germany.

THE MAJOR POETRY

STRANGE FITS OF PASSION HAVE I KNOWN

The poet will tell of a strange fit of passion that he has known, but he will tell his message only to lovers. The reason for such exclusiveness is that only the lover would understand the curious psychological responses that he has experienced while approaching Lucy's cottage ("cot"). A reading of the other four *Lucy Poems* would mean that we read this one knowing that Lucy is dead at the time the poet tells of this strange fit of passion. However, **stanza** two may be in itself enough to identify the fact that the lover tells of an incident that happened while Lucy was still living: "When she I loved looked every day / Fresh as a rose in June." On a moonlit night the poet rode towards his sweetheart's cottage. Gazing dreamily at the moon, he fell asleep on his horse, and all this while his eyes remained fixed on the moon that slipped down the sky. When suddenly the moon dropped down behind the cottage of his love, the "fond and wayward" thought slid into his mind, "If Lucy should be dead!"

Comment

Probably of all the *Lucy Poems*, the simplicity of thought and language is best in this piece. The moon becomes for the poet in his fervent love a symbol for his beloved; as with most human things, his great joy in her preciousness to him made him fear the sorrow of possible loss. The poem is most human probably for just this reason, the haunting, nudging fear of the certain limits of mortality. However simple the poem may be as a love song, it is profound at the point of commenting on the certain sorrow that comes in all human relationships regardless of how joyful they be. Indeed, one of the very nearly inevitable suggestions the poem has is that the greater the joy, the greater the sorrow. Life is a blessed gift, but it is also a vexing mystery. The coffin worm is never that far away from the flowers that celebrate birth or marriage.

Notice the traditional use of poetic figures of speech with the simile in **stanza** two, "Fresh as a rose in June...."

THE MAJOR POETRY

SHE DWELT AMONG THE UNTRODDEN WAYS

Lucy was living alone, like a violet half hidden from the eye by the stone beside which it grew, or like a solitary star, more brilliant in the heavens just because of its aloneness. The third **stanza** informs us, with a kind of abruptness, that Lucy has died.

Comment

This poem contains what is probably the most famous two figures in the whole of the Lucy group.

    A violet by a mossy stone Half hidden from the eye! - Fair as a star, when only one Is shining in the sky.

    These figures in the second **stanza** clarify what the poet is saying about Lucy in the first **stanza**. It is not that Lucy is lovely because of isolation, but in spite of it. If one talks about her isolation, one must speak of it as the isolation of rustic retirement.

Understatement as a literary device is at the highest level in this poem. One should observe through several readings of the last **stanza** the human impact-in the kind of language that people use-in the lines "But she is in her grave, and, oh, / The difference to me!" This is about as close as one can come to an antithesis to the learned eloquence of 18th-century verse. The delicacy and frailty of Lucy are suggested in this poem in the very figures that reveal her beauty. But, strangely, it is not frailty alone either. Lucy is virtually nature itself and therefore indestructible. Literally people did not know when she died because of her rustic retirement. But in a profounder sense her death was not noted because she lived so close to nature that she was very nearly absorbed in it at the time of dying-but nearly absorbed in it in life also. The message is close to being a rendering in natural terms of the theological affirmation of life in the bosom of the Father.

THE MAJOR POETRY

I TRAVELLED AMONG UNKNOWN MEN

We can feel Wordsworth's homesickness for England powerfully in this poem; let us recall that all the *Lucy Poems* were written during Wordsworth's sojourn in Germany in the winter of 1798, a stay in a foreign land that found the poet continually nostalgic for all the joys of English soil. In this poem Wordsworth is promising that when once he has returned home, he will never leave England again. Lucy figures in the poem because the poet loves England more for her being part of it. The lands in the first **stanza** are literally Germany, but more generally, any place that cuts the poet off from England and such associations with it as Lucy, who "turned her wheel / Beside an English fire." The logic of the poem is simply this; England is more precious because of Lucy, Lucy more precious because she belongs to England. The meditation of loss, which characterizes all the *Lucy Poems*, is focused here in an inseparable combination of love for country and love for beloved. England has always been the setting for the poet's joys, and Lucy has been his companion in his experience of them. English mornings revealed Lucy, English nights concealed her.

Comment

Wordsworth's patriotism is deeply humanized. It is neither vulgar nor pretentious, but, rather, deeply rooted in the simple facts of life.

Part of the nostalgia of the poem resides in the poet's inability to profess his feelings to Lucy, which would mean the same thing as professing them for England. The **theme** of the union of Lucy and the nature that surrounded her is present here again, but this time it is more her union with a particular country than with nature generally. The mornings, the nights, the bowers, the green field of the last **stanza** are all English, and not German. The nationalistic naturalism of the last **stanza** is strategically introduced by making the fire in the third **stanza** an explicitly English fire.

The contrast that is present in the other *Lucy Poems* between the joy of the poet's possessing her and the sorrow of his losing her is working at another level in this poem also; his joy at possessing England is all the greater because he can contemplate it through the telescopic lens of loss.

THE MAJOR POETRY

THREE YEARS SHE GREW IN SUN AND SHOWER

The poem has 42 lines; 35 of them are spoken by Nature when she declared, "This Child I to myself will take. . . ." Nature took a three-year-old Lucy. She was as lovely as any flower that had ever decorated the earth that nourished it, and Nature takes Lucy just because of her loveliness. Lucy will grow into a beautiful woman through the ministry of Nature - through contact with "rock and plain," "glade and bower," "floating clouds," the willow, "the motions of the Storm," "The stars of midnight," "rivulets," in summary, all the objects and moods that come within the universe of "mute insensate things." Nature predicts Lucy grown into buxom womanhood; we have nothing here of frailty; Lucy will be full, fine, fertile: "'And vital feelings of delight/ Shall rear her form to stately height, / Her virgin bosom swell. . . .'" The laws and impulses of Lucy would be those of Nature itself. Her movements would be one, however mysteriously the sympathetic magic works, with the sportive fawn. To her form would be added lightness and grace by the floating clouds and moving storms. The beauty of the dancing rivulets, the beauty of both sight and sound, will flow into Lucy's face. In the dell, Nature lives with Lucy. Perhaps only within the **metaphor** of marriage can the merging be adequately grasped. The last **stanza** should be read as a formidable "But" to what has gone before. The poet has been deceived at the length of time anticipated for Nature's ministry to Lucy, although the deception is possibly of his own making. Nature did not give the chronology of her intentions; the poet speaks in the last **stanza** as if he expected to share her life longer than was permitted. But then it may be that any time would not have been long enough, that any duration would have left him deprived, left him uttering the protest, "How soon my Lucy's race was run!"

Comment

However ironical it might seem from the poet's point of view, Nature's prophecy was absolutely fulfilled. She gave what is by implication the only possible finish to her fostering of Lucy, by taking Lucy even closer to her bosom than mortal life would permit. If one reads the poem as protest, even **metaphysical** protest, the poet might be seen softening the shock of death by avoiding the use of that word (death) and casting, rather, the whole matter in the terms of Nature's beneficent ministry. One might go so far as to read Wordsworth's poem "Nutting" as a gloss on the *Lucy Poems*. There he strikes out at Nature, although he finds her beautiful, by tearing down the branches of trees in a virginal bower. He has luxuriated in the lush loveliness of a nook of hazel trees, but then he starts up and ravages the scene as if he were rebelling against a kind of eternity that was Nature's but not his. The poems about Lucy may all be protests against the unacceptable, unmanageable fact of death by their very artistically careful avoidance of the term. But, then, what can the poet do-what can any man do-about loss? He tries to find in "This heath, this calm, and quiet scene," some resources for what all of life is in one way or another, "The memory of what has been,/ And never more will be." This poem may be read as Wordsworth's personal comment on his own cult of nature. To be alone with nature, followed to its ultimate end, is to be completely dehumanized. The poem raises the question of how can one create a balance between the human conceived in social terms and the natural in anti-social terms. No answer is given; the poet does not know.

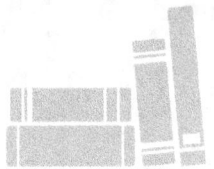

THE MAJOR POETRY

A SLUMBER DID MY SPIRIT SEAL

Lucy was so much filled with the vital beauty of life and so eternalized in the poet's association of her with nature that he could not conceive of her as subject to death. He has come to slumber in the midst of the strife of living amidst hostile elements. This slumber has sealed him off from awareness of what no one likes to be aware of-limits! He falls into the greatest danger of all, forgetfulness of the precariousness of the human condition. Somewhere beneath the "noble simplicity" of this Lucy poem there is a lash laid to the back of life itself for being what it is, and to the poet's own back for forgetting certain basic grim facts. This forgetfulness of grim facts has produced a grim **irony**: enter into the full joy of life's blessedness and find quiet peace (slumber), and you will be soon awakened by the reality of permanent sleep. The second **stanza** affirms a kind of immortality in that Lucy has become merged into the matter that rolls eternally in accord with earth's daily rotations. She is one with the atoms of "rocks, and stones, and trees."

Comment

One may talk about this poem as another of Wordsworth's own comments on his attitudes toward nature. This is hardly a sweet-tempered nature poet at work, sitting blithely on the bank of a river, chirping his own dulcet melodies in response to the bird's chirps, contemplating nature for its own sake. In a real sense he is rebuking himself for becoming aware of Lucy's humanity only after her death. The student should be careful of talking glibly about how Wordsworth (and other "Romantic" poets) love nature. He hates it at times with very nearly the passion with which he loves it at others. His optimism is often at the ebb. His attitudes toward nature are not particularly easy-going. He often uses nature to comment on "the heavy and the weary weight / Off all this unintelligible world...."

Conclusion To The Lucy Poems

The Romantics, unlike the eighteenth-century poets, were consistently interested in the particular rather than the general. All the scenes in the *Lucy Poems* are extremely particularized and are given in obviously detailed descriptions. The Romantics' interest in the particular probably stems essentially from their rejection of generalizations about Man in favor of a delighted interest in the specific individual and his specific circumstances. Wordsworth could not have written an "Essay on Man"; he could only write about Michael, Simon Lee, and Lucy.

The diversity of Wordsworth's ability as a craftsman of language can be seen in the varieties of lyrical strains in his poetry. One can usefully compare for illustration the realistic and tragic, lyricism of the *Lucy Poems*. The verbosity that in many places mars Wordsworth's poems is completely absent from the Lucy verses. They are generally agreed to be masterpieces of precision and economy in language.

THE MAJOR POETRY

LUCY GRAY

With regard to the treatment of a generally common **theme**, it may be a worthwhile procedure to read this poem immediately after the *Lucy Poems*. We have another Lucy who becomes merged into the nature that surrounds her, although the circumstances are more definitely and elaborately narrative than in any of the *Lucy Poems*.

Many a time had the poet heard of Lucy Gray. He had actually seen her once, once when he crossed the wild. Lucy's life had been spent in solitude on an expansive wasteland, "on a wide moor." Lucy Gray was " - The sweetest thing that ever grew / Beside a human door!" Nature has not changed where Lucy lived, for the fawn and the hare continue their vibrant play, but Lucy will not be seen again. The narrative of the poem begins with **stanza** four; there the quotation marks begin as the father addresses himself to Lucy. He tells her that she must go with lantern to the town and give her mother light for the walk home. Lucy replies that she will gladly go on this errand, and as if in effort to assure herself and her father of her safety, she calls attention to the fact that the morning has barely passed, for it is only two o'clock. But, it proves to be a bad omen that she sees the moon during this early afternoon hour. The father continues his work as Lucy goes blithely toward town, wantonly dispersing the snow that lies on the ground. But a storm comes up unexpectedly, and Lucy is lost. She tries strenuously to recover her directions but cannot. The parents go looking for her, shouting for her, but there is no answer. In the light of dawn the mother finds Lucy's footprint, the parents trace it over an expanse of ground but find that it disappears in the middle of a bridge of wood, a bridge located only a furlong from the door of their cottage. Some refuse to admit that Lucy had died: "....some maintain that to this day / She is a living child...." They say that she may be seen upon the lonesome moor and that her joyful step has not been slowed:

O'er rough and smooth she trips along, And never looks behind; And sings a solitary song That whistles in the wind.

Comment

The first fact about Lucy Gray that the poet names is her solitude; she is "The solitary child." She lives without contact with anyone else. In this literary **ballad** about a young girl who was " - The sweetest thing that ever grew / Beside a human door," we have one of the most obvious of Wordsworth's solitaries. She is very nearly not related at all to the human community. Involvement in the lives of other human beings is confined to her obedience to her father and to her going with willingness to meet her mother. But, she is not very like her parents either; after her death (or what they assume is her death), they suffer great anguish, but Lucy's characteristic joy remains untouched by the event her parents consider tragedy. The claim that some persons make about her, which the poet is careful to relate (last two stanzas), has for us a greater authenticity than the parent's plaintive wail, "'In heaven we all shall meet'...." The reader believes with the poet that Lucy lives. This poem becomes in the way of "We Are Seven" a two-level poem, contrasting the child's oblivion to the limits of mortality to the painfully vivid awareness of the adult mind. A number of Wordsworth's poems concern the fading of "the vision splendid" "into the light of common day." The "Ode: Intimations of Immortality," one of Wordsworth's most famous (and most excellent) poems, is the poet's attempt to find a meaningful replacement in a future direction for the lost "visionary gleam" of his youth. Lucy Gray is, of course, in great degree William Wordsworth; she is poet too; or, better, she is what William Wordsworth would wish to be, a creature unbattered by the recognitions and experiences of an historical consciousness, a consciousness that tells of life's limits and life's ends. She is interestingly described in one **stanza** with the same poetic figure that Wordsworth uses for himself in "Tintern Abbey." In **stanza** seven Wordsworth say the mountain roe is not blither than Lucy. Compare these lines from "Tintern Abbey":

And so I dare to hope, Though changed, no doubt, from what I was when first I came among these hills; when like a roe I bounded o'er the mountains, by the sides Of the deep rivers, and the lonely streams, Wherever nature led. . . .

In no other poem by Wordsworth is the union of a solitary figure with nature so evident as it is in "Lucy Gray." In very nearly the classical way that mystics become in a final stage blended with the Godhead they yearn toward, Lucy Gray merges with nature. She does not die in a way that is marked by definite historical action; the mystic does not have historical relatedness to the Divine either. The footmarks that the parents trace farther and farther into nature stop only as a blending into-strikingly and tellingly in the very middle of the bridge. The very geographical point that Lucy has reached in nature is not, deliberately not, an end of anything. Having made the transition (one may say into the Platonic One), she does not look back with nostalgia, as her time-bound parents would; rather,

O'er rough and smooth she trips along, And never looks behind; And sings a solitary song That whistles in the wind.

 Obviously in this poem Wordsworth is using the **ballad** technique. The **rhyme** scheme is very similar to that of the established tradition in ballad form. Note that in "Lucy Gray" we have a b a b; the **ballad** stanza traditionally is a b c b. Further, the abrupt change from narrative to dialogue (from **stanza** three to stanza four) is a traditional device in the **ballad** form, as is the abrupt change in the plot of the narrative (from **stanza** two to three, and from stanza seven to stanza eight). The subject matter of the **ballad** tends to be more tragic than not, but one should be sensitive to the deeper dimensions of the tragic elements in "Lucy Gray." One should note the departure from traditional **ballad** approach also in that in "Lucy Gray" the story is told in the first person, and the poet's feelings are revealed to us; in the traditional **ballad** the narrative is highly dramatic and is presented mainly through dialogue with no first person, singular or plural, allowed. The lyrical quality in "Lucy Gray" is in great measure the result of the poet's use of the first person. Perhaps this is one of the important things that Wordsworth and Coleridge meant by the term "lyrical ballads," the use of the old ballad technique but with the modifications and modernizations of adding the more subjective and lyrical dimension.

THE MAJOR POETRY

THE TWO APRIL MORNINGS

This is one of the Matthew poems. They have more of a dramatic structure than either the *Lucy Poems* or "Lucy Gray." The nostalgia of the Matthew poems is focused away from the poet, unlike the poems about Lucy and Lucy Gray. They are not as subjective; the poet's involvement does not seem to be as personal. Matthew is thinking of the past in both "The Two April Mornings" and "The Fountain." Who is Matthew? He is obviously not the Matthew of "Expostulation and Reply," the Matthew said to have his historical prototype in William Hazlitt.

The important distinction between the Matthew of "Expostulation and Reply" and the one of the Matthew poems is that Matthew in "The Two April Mornings" and in "The Fountain" is a man who obviously delights in the outdoors.

In "The Two April Mornings" the poet and Matthew have gone together on a walking trip, "to pass / A day among the hills" in merry travel. The morning sun, "bright and red," augurs a beautiful day for their excursion. The poet (**stanza** four) considers the day well-begun. But Matthew, the village schoolmaster, this man of "glittering grey" hair, a blithe man, suddenly interrupts their walk, and when he stops the second time, he answers the poet's question as to the cause of a sad sigh he has uttered:

"Yon cloud with that long purple cleft Brings fresh into my mind A day like this which I have left Full thirty years behind.'

The sights that Matthew sees as he looks around him, particularly the purple cleft in the cloud and the colors in the sky, remind him of an incident from thirty years ago when during an outing he stopped beside his daughter's grave. We learn from Matthew that his daughter Emma had died when she was scarcely nine years old, and that he loved her more on the day when he stopped in the churchyard than he had ever loved her before. She was his pride and the pride of those who lived in the vale, and he compares her joy in living to that of the nightingale. Matthew tells the poet that as he turned to leave Emma's grave, he met "Beside the churchyard yew" a beautiful, joyful girl whom it was a delight to behold. She tripped as lightly as a fountain's bubbling water, and she appeared as joyful as a dancing wave. The last two **stanzas** of the poem present a response from Matthew that the poet listening to him (and the reader) does not expect-we feel that Matthew did not expect it in himself either. As he beholds this lovely and joyful girl, he unavoidably utters "a sigh of pain"; the **irony** is that we would have expected Matthew, after what he said about his Emma, to wish this girl were his, a replacement for his lost daughter. But he looks twice at her, and the second look confirms his feeling that he does not want her.

Comment

The poem protests the limits of mortality, the shades of the prison-house that fall over all of us. One may take the poem to mean that Matthew could never find any human creature, however beautiful and joyful, to take the place of his Emma. More likely, considering the tone of rebellion in the next-to-the-last **stanza**, Matthew is unwilling to enter again into the kind of human relationship that has given him such agony. When Matthew sees the "blooming Girl, whose hair was wet / With points of morning dew," he does not wish her as his own because he has had enough of human suffering, at least that kind that comes from losing a child so near and so dear. Perhaps the "bough / Of wilding" that the poet remembers Matthew holding on that day when they went walking and when Matthew told his story, is intended as a symbol of contrast to the rod and line that Matthew held on the other April morning, thirty years previous to the morning on which he and the poet were walking companions. The poem is philosophy in its suggestion that when one enters into human relationship, one must be aware of the full load of joy and sorrow one will carry; perhaps the ancillary suggestion is that refusing the burden is refusing to be human.

THE MAJOR POETRY

THE FOUNTAIN

The subtitle identifies the poem as conversation. The situation is not a journey but leisure "beneath a spreading oak...." The poet and Matthew are talking "with open heart, and tongue / Affectionate and true...." The poet is young, Matthew is seventy-two. One might expect, therefore that the poet as youth will learn something about life from a source of greater maturity. But, the poet does not ask for truth; rather, the first element of dialogue in the poem is in the poet's request to Matthew that the schoolmaster join him in the singing of a **ballad**, or that Matthew quote to him his "half-mad thing of witty rhymes." Matthew refuses any such jocund exercise. He, rather, takes the opportunity to discourse philosophically on the fountain and the stream, on the free blackbirds that sing, to contrast his present state with what he was on a long-past "delightful day," and on the fact that however much he is loved, he is not loved enough. The poet must wait until they depart from the oak tree and go on their way to hear Matthew's odd poem.

Comment

This poem may be intended as a companion poem to "The Two April Mornings," or the other way around. The focus of the poem is Matthew's discussion of the "heavy laws" that press upon human creatures, as contrasted to the freedom that the stream and the birds enjoy. Matthew first contrasts his present state of old age and loneliness with the stream that goes racing merrily by; nothing checks the flow of the stream, but many things check the flow of human life. Second, the contrast with the birds that sing is that they accept the limits of life without rebellion; "'With Nature never do they wage / A foolish strife...'"; they have happy youth plus a beautiful and free old age. To the contrary, human creatures contrast the deprivations of old age with the fulfillments of youth (**stanza** seven); human creatures "wear a face of joy" too often not because of their present fulfillments, but, rather, because they recall in present pain the joy that has past; the man who once felt such deep love for his kindred that are now laid in the earth is the man who must in his present feel such deep sorrow; one never experiences enough love from his fellows, however great their love may be: the human condition necessarily means that one must suffer-to be human is to be deprived - there is no escape! The possibility that "The Fountain" is intended to be a companion poem to "The Two April Mornings" is perhaps most evident in that Matthew rejects flatly the poet's offer that he become a son to Matthew, an adopted son who will help to deflect the "heavy laws" under which Matthew suffers. As the Matthew of "The Two April Mornings" refused the little girl as a possible daughter to replace the lost Emma, so Matthew in "The Fountain" refuses the poet's offer to become his son. The departure that Matthew makes with the poet from their leisure place of talk beneath the oak emphasizes Matthew's rejection of the poet's sonship. In the desperation of sorrow over what is lost, Matthew takes the only road out, the one that Byron takes in Don Juan, laughter at that which could drive one to insanity and self-destruction. The clock and the chimes of **stanza** four have become in the last **stanza** "the crazy old church-clock, / And the bewildered chimes." If time and the events that it imposes upon human kind are ultimately a mystery, enough so to be crazy and bewildered, then the only human response that can ensure the continuation of life in the midst of the mystery is to comment on the mystery with mockery. Matthew responds to the "blank misgivings" of time and its agonizing mysteries (loss, disappointment, age and sickness, suffering, death) with laughter, a "half-mad thing of witty rhymes."

WORDSWORTH'S SOLITARIES

The child in "We Are Seven," Martha Ray in "The Thorn," "Simon Lee," and Lucy of the *Lucy Poems,* Lucy Gray are typical Wordsworthian solitaries. But even more exactly representative of the class are the Old Cumberland Beggar, Michael, and the old leech-gatherer of "Resolution and Independence." All of these characters live close to nature and derive their dignity from the natural elements. They lead their lives as if they were the wind or the stream. There is a certain quality about them that makes it impossible for us to put them indoors. In them we can find Wordsworth grappling with the inherent tension between the merely natural and the purely human.

THEMES

We find in the poems dedicated to solitaries such emphases and **themes** as (1) the integral importance of persons surrounded by circumstances unlike those the mass of mankind know, (2) the inseparable relationship to all of life that solitaries have even though they are solitary, (3) the brutal conditions and events in life that can make solitaries of persons who once belonged, (4) the human sympathy that can be stirred in the hearts of others, those who behold the solitaries.

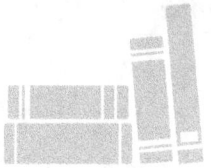

THE MAJOR POETRY

THE OLD CUMBERLAND BEGGAR

There is in this poem political reaction, reaction to such legislation as that of Benthamite utilitarianism, and that of the Poor Relief Act of 1795. There were in Wordsworth's day utilitarian movements against beggars. The Poor Relief Act of 1795 provided for relief for beggars through providing monies out of parish treasuries. Wordsworth was against any such institutional programs and opposed them as the unwanted, inappropriate meddling of state legislation in private lives. The poem should be read as being in part a direct attack on legislative efforts to get beggars into poorhouses.

Lines 1-21

The poet first sees the Beggar who is the subject of the poem as he sits with his bag of "scraps and fragments" given him by the women of the village. Surrounded by a solitary natural scene, his staff placed nearby, the old Beggar eats his solitary meal; the solitude is broken only by birds that come to pick up the scraps that his palsied hand cannot help but drop onto the ground.

Lines 22-43

The poet affirms that he has known this old Beggar for many years; he says that the old "solitary Man" was old even during his (the poet's) childhood, so old then that he does not seem any older now. The Beggar has for all the poet's life had about him the appearance and character of the eternal. The poet gives three instances of the high regard in which others hold the Beggar. The man who comes on horseback by the beggar does not merely toss his alms upon the ground, but, rather, he dismounts and puts his contribution carefully in the Beggar's hand. Next, the woman at the toll-gate quits her work at her wheel and lifts the latch for the Beggar that he may pass. The post-boy will not utter unkind words at the old man even if he must turn to the roadside in his conveyance in order not to strike the Beggar.

Lines 44-66

These lines describe the slow movement of the "Poor Traveller." The old Beggar sees only one small patch of the earth, and he seldom takes any account of the objects that might come within his narrowed purview, whether straw, or scattered leaf, or nailmarks left in the road by passing wheels. In these lines the poet's description of the Beggar make him nearly still; his near stillness makes him seem only another object in nature. As he walks his feet hardly stir the dust on the road.

Lines 67-161

After giving us to understand how old and helpless the beggar is, the poet tells us that this solitary should not be deemed useless.

He addresses to the Statesmen of the world (the legislators who make laws to rid the countryside of the mendicants),

But deem not this Man useless. . . . ye Who are so restless in your wisdom, ye Who have a broom still ready in your hands To rid the world of nuisances; ye proud, Heart-swoln, while in your pride ye contemplate Your talents, power, or wisdom, deem him not A burthen of the earth!

It is the law of Nature that everything that lives is holy and has a value of its own. This is the heart of the poem with regard to the philosophical basis of its message:

'Tis Nature's law That none, the meanest of created things, Of forms created the most vile and brute, The dullest or most noxious, should exist Divorced from good-a spirit and pulse of good, A life and soul, to every mode of being Inseparably linked.

MAJOR POINTS

Two emphases here: first, the Beggar is priceless just because he is unlike the rest of men; second, the Beggar, whether others wish to recognize it or not, is indivisibly linked to all human souls in the great chain of humanity. The Beggar's ministry to humankind is in the inspiration that he provides to charity, love, and sympathy. As the old Beggar goes from house to house, the villagers find themselves reminded of past deeds of charity that they might otherwise forget in the easily-increasing insensitivity of routine living and the passage of time. The indigence of the Beggar compels the villagers to acts of love, and the pleasure that flows from this moves them to the further desire to do the good. Even the lofty minds of the world, "authors of delight / And happiness," who spread abroad the light of goodness in the world, often found "That first mild touch of sympathy and thought" in such a wanderer as this solitary Beggar. Even those who diligently refrain from the evil, who read the Ten Commandments with scrupulous attention and obedience, who follow in all ways the moral law of their country, even these will find in relationship with such an one as the Old Cumberland Beggar a warmth in their souls that could never come from mere lawfulness. One of his neighbors, the poet tells, gave to the old Beggar duly every Friday, although she could scarcely afford to give what she offered, and she found as a consequence that her hope in heaven was contemplated with more exhilarated heart.

Lines 162-197

The poet concludes with an appeal in behalf of the Old Cumberland Beggar, that he left free by man to wander where he will, unconfined by "House, misnamed of Industry," that "pent-up din" the poorhouse: "Let him be free of mountain solitudes; / . . . . . . / . . . let him, where and when he will, sit down. . . ." These closing lines of the poem assert again the dual value of the Beggar's life: he is precious because of what he is as a human being, in and of himself, and he is precious because of the prompting he gives to the villagers, prompting of them. "To tender offices and pensive thoughts." The appeal to society for the freedom of the Beggar reaches its most concentrated focus in the poet's plea that he not only be left alone, but that he be left alone with all the fierceness of the natural elements. To protect him from "that vast solitude to which / The tide of things has borne him" would be to deprive him of the peculiar identity that is uniquely his. The poet appeals, "let his blood / Struggle with frosty air and winter snows. . . ." Finally when death comes to him let the old Beggar die "in the eye of Nature," which is where he has made his mortal life.

Comment

There are some critics who consider this poem a failure (or a near failure) because of the quality of the **blank verse** used, its slow movement and heavy tone. Some say that the **blank verse** in this poem does not have the vitality of the verse in such poems as "Michael" And "Tintern Abbey." Critics also often consider the poem too preachy. The moralizing is too direct, they say. The poet's stand for the utilitarian approach, some say, is too obvious in that it says too plainly, Let the Beggar have his life for what his life contributes to ours. Charles Lamb, one of Wordsworth's contemporaries, found the moral of the poem too obvious. Wordsworth, on the other hand, sent copies of it to some British statesmen, hoping to win them to the side of his cause. Wordsworth's democratic beliefs and temperament are very explicit in this poem, however inferior as poetry the work may be. He takes a very humble figure and bestows upon him all the grandeur possible. This is the first of Wordsworth's great solitaries. His poetry, as already suggested, frequently has such figures, persons who live in such a close relationship with nature that they become actually merged with it. We feel them to be so inseparably a part of nature that they seem as immutable as the natural order to which they belong. It is what Wordsworth does with the Old Cumberland Beggar that is significant; the person is no original invention on his part. Both the countryside of England and the literature of 1780s and 1790s were peopled with such pathetic figures as the old Beggar, men of former military service who had been discharged, women either widowed or deserted, persons reduced to poverty by misfortune or mismanaged economic affairs.

THE MAJOR POETRY

MICHAEL

Wordsworth calls this "A Pastoral Poem." We should give more than passing notice to the use of the word Pastoral in the subtitle. Wordsworth is explicitly challenging the reader to compare "Michael" as a pastoral poem to the conventional pastoral poems in English (and Greek) literature. The poet is consciously, deliberately, devotedly rejecting the Arcadians and other artificial shepherds of 18th-century poetry and is presenting instead the real shepherds of the Lake District in England. The assault against established pastoral poetry is direct Just because his shepherds are genuine people living in a particular geographical place (and the geographical particularity of "Michael" requires no argument in defense), and not fanciful figures who tend to literary sheep on an imaginative countryside, Wordsworth felt free to consider his poem (in sending it to Fox) a piece of political literature. There is no truck in Wordsworth with pastoral poetry from the ancients.

Lines 1-39

In a steep, narrow valley, made secret by the arrangement of the mountains, there is beside a brook a very simple and humble object which has an interesting story. This, the poet says, is his only reason for making mention of the Dell where "a few sheep, with rocks and stones, and kites / That overhead are sailing in the sky" make for utter solitude. The story he will tell, he clarifies, is "unenriched with strange events . . . " The poet tells that the story came to him when he was yet unconcerned with books; it is the first such story he heard about the shepherds whom he loved, not for their sake but, rather, because of the places where they lived, "for the fields and hills / Where was their occupation and abode." The story came to him at the time in his life when the objects of nature were humanizing him, when Nature was, through her sights and sounds, creating in him the capacity to be sympathetic with the feelings of other human beings, causing him to "think / . . . . . . / On man, the heart of man, and human life." He says that he will tell the story "For the delight of a new natural hearts," and "for the sake / Of youthful Poets . . . ."

Lines 40-77

The narrative begins at line 40. The poet describes Michael. He lived "Upon the forest-side in Grasmere vale." He was old at the time the poet knew him; he had a stout heart; he was strong in the resources of muscle and mind; he was unusually sensitive to the various tasks of his work; he had rejoiced in being alone with the forms and forces of nature; he had found in green valleys, streams, rocks, fields, hills, and while among the animals he cared for, truths that are perhaps not to be found in other places and experiences-so the tone of this section of the poem would seem to suggest. One of the most important reasons that Michael is unique is that "he learned the meaning of all winds, / Of blasts of every tone . . . ." He responded to storms that drove others to shelter; ". . . he had been alone / Amid the heart of many thousand mists. . . ." Michael had lived all his life in intimate contact with nature and had become intimately knowledgeable of its mind and spirit, all its weather and its lore. His heart had learned to be filled with joy and awe because of his intermingling with the natural elements.

Lines 78-139

Michael had not lived his life alone, though the previous lines of the poem might point in that direction. With him was his wife, Isabel, twenty years his junior, and their son, Luke, born to the pair after Michael was in his old age. All the members of Michael's household led industrious, productive lives. The introduction of the wife includes a comment on her "stirring life," and Luke is first named with his "two brave sheep-dogs" that have followed him in the shepherd's work through many storms. Not only did this family labor in the daylight hours. When the sun had gone away, they would continue to work by the light of an old lamp, "Surviving comrade of uncounted hours," which had come, through its long hours of service, to cause the cottage to have the name in the neighborhood of "The Evening Star." The lamp that burned for many hours into the night had become a symbol of the kind of thrifty life that Michael and his family lived.

Lines 140-206

These sixty-six lines tell of Michael's feelings for his son, Luke. As one might expect, Michael's love for Luke was greater because the child had been born to him and to his wife when the old shepherd was very advanced in years. Luke was more dear to him than was his wife, for Luke had brought to Michael "forward-looking thoughts," hope for spiritual vigor, perhaps hopefulness for life beyond the life of this world. Luke had been born after those years when romance and the passionate love of youthful yearning had become softened into the quiet companionship of home, and heart, and hearth-side tasks. Michael had cared for Luke with even mother's devotion, so great was his love. While Luke was still a child, "ere yet the Boy / Had put on boy's attire," Michael loved to have his son near him as he worked. When Luke reached five years of age, "A healthy Lad, and carried in his cheek / Two steady roses that were five years old," Michael made for him a shepherd's staff. Luke began then to be a shepherd, though he was "Something between a hindrance and a help . . . ." The companionship between father and son reached its full flower when Luke became ten years old, could go with Michael to the heights, and "could stand / Against the mountain blasts" with him. The objects in nature that Michael had always loved became to him dearer, now that Luke could share them with him: " . . . from the Boy there came / Feelings and emanations - things which were / Light to the sun and music to the wind . . . ." Luke grew up in his father's sight, "With light upon him from his father's eyes," and at eighteen Luke had become his father's "comfort and daily hope."

Lines 207-282

The lives of Michael's family are interrupted by "Distressful tidings." This part of the poem tells of the problem that has developed and Michael's plans to cope with it. A number of years before, Michael had agreed to be responsible for debt or damage that his nephew might suffer. The nephew had family characteristics: he was industrious and came to possess through his industry "ample means." But he has been pressed by "unforeseen misfortunes." Michael is bound to take up the slack in his sagging fortunes. The forfeiture will cost Michael one-half of the estate his seventy years have been spent to secure. When he had summoned up his slackened fortitude, Michael first considered selling "A portion of his patrimonial fields." But his second thought is to send Luke to the city, to the city necessarily, for there Michael has a kinsman who will put Luke to work, and Luke can through hard work and thrift quickly repair the damaged finances of the family. The land on which Michael's family works could not supply the necessary return to meet the demands of the debt. Michael will not sell the lands (remember Wordsworth's letter to Fox); he could not rest in his grave if he did. In what is without doubt some of the best Wordsworth's dialogue, Michael explains the plan to his wife, Isabel. Isabel recalls the story of Richard Bateman, a poor parish-boy, who went to London, found a master, went across the seas, grew rich, became a philanthropist and sent home marble for a chapel. Isabel's thoughts of young Bateman brighten her countenance, whereupon Michael directs her to prepare Luke's garments for his trip to the city.

Lines 282-303

Michael in his eagerness to dispatch this harrowing obligation has wished that Luke could leave immediately, but Isabel works morning and night for five days to get Luke properly prepared for the beginning of this new responsibility. She is glad for the Sabbath day to interrupt her work, for she has been conscious for the past two nights that Michael has had troubled sleep. On the morning of Sunday, she sees in Michael's face that all his hopes are gone; she finally says that Luke must not go: "Thou must not go: / We have no other Child but thee to lose, / None to remember-do not go away, / For if thou leave thy Father he will die,'" But Luke encourages both mother and father, and that evening their hope is restored; they sit with glad hearts around the fire.

Lines 304-322

A letter comes from Michael's kinsman in the city. He writes that he will do all he can to care for Luke and to make his efforts successful. He asks that Luke come to him right away. The letter brings such joyful tidings that they read it ten times at least. Luke's heart is proud; Isabel goes to show their neighbors the kinsman's warm and affectionate invitation; Michael in his reassurance says that Luke will leave on the morrow.

Lines 323-430

The evening before Luke leaves for the city, Michael takes him "Near the tumultuous brook of Greenhead Ghyll." (Wordsworth had begun the poem with the identification of this brook. To return to it at this point is to identify this as a midway point in the poem.) In this place, in the "deep valley," Michael had intended to build a Sheep-fold. Even before the news arrived about his nephew, he had collected the stones needed for the job and had placed them by the side of the brook. They waited there to be arranged into a meaningful form. When father and son arrived at this spot, Michael spoke to Luke of times gone by, how his son had been to him a promise and a joy in every day. Michael confides that the purpose of this remembrance of their "two histories" is to provide Luke with support for future times. Michael first tells of the great love he had for his son while he slept away the first two days after his birth, while he sang at his mother's breast. Michael recalls next how they have among the hills whereon their shepherding was done shared all pleasures mutually, how in being a kind father to Luke, he has but done what his parents did for him, how the land that Luke goes forth to liberate from the demand of the family debt is the land of their Forefathers and how it could not endure the sovereignty of other masters. Michael asks Luke's forgiveness if he has made a wrong decision in sending the boy away. Pointing to the stones that he had gathered for the Sheep-fold, Michael says that it was a work they both should have shared, but that he wishes Luke on the eve of his departure to lay one stone in the spirit of "good hope," that both of them "may live / Too see a better day." The Sheep-fold will become a covenant between them. Michael says to Luke that though he is eighty-four he will resume the management of the land and the flock as he managed them before Luke came to him. In asking Luke to lay the corner-stone of the Sheep-fold, Michael offers to his son a reminder of his love for him, of the life of his forefathers who in their innocence sought to do good deeds. Michael says that this act of covenantal bond between them will give Luke a point of resource to return to in those coming days when he will be tempted to evil:

"and hereafter, Luke, When thou art gone away, should evil men Be thou companions, think of me, my Son, And of this moment; hither turn thy thoughts, And God will strengthen thee. . . ."

Luke lays the first stone for the Sheep-fold, as Michael requested him to do, Michael feels great grief at Luke's leaving, he kisses his son, they return home to fearful sleep, Luke leaves the next morning, and the neighbors wave good wishes as he goes with bold face into the world, to London to meet his kinsman.

Lines 431-447

The news that comes to The Evening Star from Luke is at first very good news. Michael's Kinsman wrote of Luke's "well-doing"; Luke himself wrote letters that were full of love and "wondrous news," letters that Isabel called "The prettiest letters that were ever seen.'" Michael had taken up the work of the farm and was carrying it on in the son's absence; whenever he could find some time he would go to the brook of Green-head Ghyll and work at the Sheep-fold. Luke in the city eventually fell into evil ways, brought down "ignominy and shame" and himself, and finally had to escape the tightening net of implication by going to another country. Wordsworth's description of Luke's fall is a marvel of poetic compression; observe that he tells the whole of Luke's degeneration in six lines:

Meantime Luke began To slacken in his duty; and, at length, He in the dissolute city gave himself To evil courses: ignominy and shame Fell on him, so that he was driven at last To seek a hiding-place beyond the seas.

Lines 448-482

Luke's dissolution of character becomes in time the reason for the loss of The Evening Star and the farm on which it had stood. Michael died seven years after Luke had fallen away from his family; Isabel survived Michael by three years. The land of Michael's ancestors, the land that he had sought vainly to preserve for his son and coming generations, passed into other ownership, and great changes were made on the estate. The father had returned for solace to the nature to which he had from early years belonged: "Among the rocks / He went, and still looked up to sun and cloud, / And listened to the wind...." He worked as shepherd and occasionally (though not with much heart) put stones on the Sheep-fold. There remains now only the unfinished structure by the brook and the oak that had stood beside the cottage door to identify the love and family that was but is no more.

Comment

Of all the solitaries that stride with dignity through Wordsworth's poems, however stooped these persons might be with human care, Michael is the one of greatest dignity. No one thinks of Wordsworth as having failed in this poem, certainly not in characterization. In his fundamental aloneness and heroic stature, Michael carries with him many reminders of the stories of the Biblical Patriarchs. Were he Hebraic rather than English to his marrow, were he historically oriented in the Old Testament demands, rather than naturalistically oriented to sun and cloud and wind, he might very easily serve as the Knight of Faith, Abraham, who goes up the mountain to sacrifice his son Isaac. In fact, it seems that Wordsworth is trying deliberately to create a deeply religious ethos in this poem; besides such obvious matters as Michael's character, and Luke's name, there is the use of the word covenant in the reason for building the Sheep-fold. But, as suggested, there is an important distinction between covenant in "Michael" and covenant in Biblical relationships; Michael can return to his deep union with nature when all else has failed-something no Biblical Patriarch could ever do. The Old Testament attitudes toward God do not permit anything so vague as a relationship with God as a Divine Spirit that moves in and through nature. Michael is not broken by this kind of historical particularity; he can go back up the mountain and live with mist and wind.

COURAGE

The typical Wordsworthian courage is not manifested through acts of assertion and aggression; on the contrary, if finds expression in acts of endurance of deep suffering (compare the Old Cumberland Beggar, Martha Ray in "The Thorn," and the leech-gatherer in "Resolution and Independence"). Michael's particular kind of heroism is that he sticks to life even after he has nothing to live for; it is in this trait that he most resembles the Patriarchs,, for they stick to their relationship with God even though their lives may become absurd.

WISDOM

There is throughout "Michael" the **theme** that the old shepherd has learned the deepest wisdom he knows through immediate, actual, active contact with nature. Again and again the poet uses images from nature to emphasize the link. But, it is important to point out that Wordsworth is too much a humanist to let the natural predominate over the human. Ultimately, the figure of Michael towers above even nature. In this he is a kind of Representative Man, Man reduced to his essentials. That Man is portrayed in "Michael" not as an aristocrat but as shepherd of course identifies the poem as profoundly democratic in purpose.

DIALOGUE

About 125 lines of the poem are dialogue, and as dialogue, these lines are probably the most excellent that Wordsworth ever wrote. We may indeed wonder at times if this is the "language really used by men," but it is certainly not the established **diction** that had been used in so much of 18th-century poetry. There is in the dialogue in "Michael" a distance created between the events the poem is about and the telling of them. The story of the poem is really told by the people who were Michael's neighbors, and the poet is spokesman for them. This distancing helps to give the poem a nobility in tone.

PROTEST

"Michael" is one of the poems from the corpus of English Romantic poetry that makes the protest against the city in loudest terms. God dwells in the country; evil dwells in the city. Notice that Wordsworth uses the adjective dissolute to specify the character of the place that ruined Luke, and in the process of ruining him that ruined his whole family and heritage.

Against the poorhouse that threatens life in "The Old Cumberland Beggar," there is in "Michael" The Evening Star that teems with human industry. This is the Wordsworthian social, political protest against the defamation of the humble.

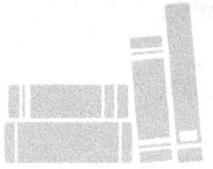

THE MAJOR POETRY

RESOLUTION AND INDEPENDENCE

Wordsworth's sister Dorothy records in her Journal the meeting that she and her brother had with the old leech-gatherer who is the subject of this poem. That entry is from 3 October 1800. Among the characteristics she names are the following: "an old man almost double"; "he carried a bundle"; "His face was interesting. He had dark eyes and a long nose"; "He was of Scotch parents, but had been born in the army"; his wife had borne him ten children, all of which were dead now except one who was a sailor; "His trade was to gather leeches, but now leeches were scarce, and he had not strength for it"; "He lived by begging"; "He had been hurt in driving a cart"; "He felt no pain till he recovered from his first insensibility."

The incident of the poem, then, was in 1800, but the creative idea did not occur to Wordsworth until April, 1802. Remember his comment "that poetry is the spontaneous overflow of powerful feelings: it takes its origin from emotion recollected in tranquility. . . ."

Lines 1-49 (Stanzas 1-7)

The poet establishes in the first two **stanzas** the mood of nature when he travelled on the moor. The tenses can be confusing. Wordsworth begins in the simple past tense, but he changes after the first two lines to the present. Again he changes the tense in **stanza** three to the past, but the past serves here the uses of the present in the sense of active recollection of past emotion in present tranquillity. The But at the beginning of **stanza** four introduces the contrast that exists between the joy of nature and the dejection of the poet. The time that he recalls was one of a rising sun, "calm and bright," singing birds "in the distant woods," the "pleasant noise of waters" in the air, the world teeming with "All things that love the sun," the grass jeweled with rain-drops, the hare running in his glee. But the poet's morning is one subjectively of dejection; on this morning did "fears and fancies" come upon him profusely. In the midst of "the sky-lark warbling in the sky," he likens himself unto "the playful hare": "Even such a happy Child of earth am I [the poet says]; / Even as these blissful creatures do I fare; / Far from the world I walk, and from all care...." This is the joyous side of his life-so far, so good. But, in the midst of the joy, he thinks of that other kind of day that might come to him, that day of "Solitude, pain of heart, distress, and poverty." He recalls (**stanza** 6) how his life has been as "a summer mood," how the sustenance of life in all its nourishing variations has come to him so gratuitously. But, then he thinks also of the possibility that it will not continue so for one who takes no practical thought for his own care and keep. The question is, how long will nature continue to give freely to one who does not with diligent responsibility harvest grain for the garner of future days: "But how can He [in this case the poet himself] expect that others should / Build for him, sow for him, and at his call / Love him, who for himself will take no heed at all?" The poet thinks of himself as poet, one endowed with the blessings of poetic mind and spirit, and in the contemplation of his own privileged, joyous place in life, there comes to his mind the names of Thomas Chatterton and Robert Burns, poets in the English tradition that Wordsworth would admire. The association that he makes of himself with them is at one and the same time joyous and imminent: "We Poets in our youth begin in gladness; / But thereof come in the end despondency and madness." The universal joy of the poet's life is contemplated in range of potential sorrow. Poets like Chatterton and Burns were the most joyful of men, but later life spelled for them another tale.

Lines 50-77 (Stanzas 8-11)

The Now at the beginning of **stanza** 8 (line 50) marks a turning point in the poem. From this juncture to the end, the poet will tell how he learned what we find in the title, resolution and independence, and he learns significantly not from a graduate of Oxford, not from nobleman, not from legislator, not even from the owner of an estate-but, rather, he learns from a wanderer, a man who has subsisted on the gathering of leeches, a man who is now a beggar. As the poet thinks his "untoward thoughts" about life and struggles with all their depressing suggestions, he meets in a lonely place, "Beside a pool bare to the eye of heaven," a solitary man, the poet says "The oldest man he seemed that ever wore grey hairs." The poet interprets his meeting with him to be verily a gift of Divine Grace. **Stanza** nine is Wordsworth's long **simile** (almost **epic** in length and complexity) for the old solitary. The purpose of the **simile** is to describe the leech gatherer as alive but almost not alive. Wordsworth compares him to "a huge stone.../ Couched on the bald top of an eminence," and to "a sea-beast crawled forth" through using the sea-beast as **simile** for the stone. The old man is virtually one with the scene amidst which he sits; he has very nearly become one with nature: "Motionless as a cloud the old Man stood,/ That heareth not the loud winds when they call...." The encounter reveals to the poet a man of great age, bent double, "feet and head / Coming together in life's pilgrimage...." He looks as if he might be made taut in his bent posture by the tight strain of some past suffering, rage, or sickness. The poet is picturing him as very nearly supernatural, at least somehow beyond the usual scope of human experience: he seemed to bear "A more than human weight...." **Stanza** sixteen will further draw such a portrait, as will **stanza** nineteen.

Lines 78-105 (Stanzas 12-15)

The old man finally moves. The poet sees him stir the waters by which he stands and then looks with fixed scrutiny into the pond, "which he conned [con: to study, peruse, or scan], / As if he had been reading in a book...." The poet greets him, and the old Man makes a gentle answer, "In courteous speech which forth he slowly drew...." Wordsworth uses the whole stanza fourteen to describe his speech, "lofty utterance," "stately speech." The poet (lines 88 & 89) asks him what is his occupation and suggests that the place in which he dwells may be too lonely for such a person as he. The old Man identifies his work as leech-gathering; this is why he is in such a lonely place. He must, "being old and poor," find his subsistence here, though the work may be "hazardous and wearisome." He depends on God's Providence to help him find lodging. But in all, he can be sure that he gains "an honest maintenance," however much he may have to roam "From pond to pond . . . from moor to moor."

Lines 106-119 (Stanzas 16 & 17)

The poet's responses to the old leech-gatherer are told. While the old Man had been answering his question about employment and placement in so lonely a setting, the poet becomes absorbed in the strange aspects of him who speaks. He loses the detail of the answer the leech-gatherer is making; he cannot divide his words one from another. Lines 109-112 contain the essence of the poet's articulation of his feelings. They should be read carefully and compared to other passages in Wordsworth's poetry where he attempts to give voice to experience that is very close to mystical absorption. Observe here that the poet finds himself absorbed in the being of the solitary:

And the whole body of the Man did seem Like one whom I had met with in a dream; Or like a man from some far region sent, To give me human strength, by apt admonishment.

But the poet's dejection returns. He thinks again the heavy thoughts of fear, of resistant, recalcitrant desperation, "Cold, pain, and labour, and all fleshly ills," and of those poets who have been mighty, but who have died in misery. He yearns to find some message of strength and hope in the leech-gather's words, so he asks again, "'How is it that you live, and what is it you do?'"

Lines 120-126 (Stanza 18)

The leech-gatherer repeats the nature of his work, but he adds that whereas he once could gather the object of his industry easily, he now because of the growing scarcity of leeches must travel more extensively-still he perseveres.

Lines 127-133 (Stanza 19)

The poet relates more of his private, unspoken response to the old Man. Again it happens that his mind wanders, as in **stanza 16**, while the leech-gatherer is answering his question. The poet pictures him as even more a solitary than he is in his present state; the poet's imagination working on the figure before him makes of the wandering solitary very nearly a transcendent being, silent and eternal: "In my mind's eye [the poet affirms] I seemed to see him pace / About the weary moors continually, / Wandering about alone and silently." The poet is troubled by his own imaginative responses to the Man before him, but not troubled in a bad sense. This is the ministry of fear that we find so often in Wordsworth's work.

Lines 134-140 (Stanza 20)

The leech-gatherer's resolution and independence is obvious to the poet in the way he moves from his economically precarious condition to more cheerful utterances. The old Man before the poet is obviously a person of firm mind, however decrepit he might in appearance seem. He remains in the midst of whatever misfortune the society of man or isolation with the bare elements bring him, a person of kind demeanor and stately bearing. The poet compares himself to the leech-gatherer and scorns himself for his dejection. He takes the old Man into his memory as an anchor point for future days and asks that God will help him to preserve what he has learned: "'God,' said I, 'be my help and stay secure; I'll think of the leech-gatherer on the lonely moor!'"

Comment

As suggested in other places in this study, most of Wordsworth's solitaries live as a part of the nature in which they move. There is the effect in this poem of the leech-gatherer going in and out of nature; the poet is for a time aware of him as a person confronting him face-to-face, but then he loses touch with him, as if he had blended back into the nature out of which he had momentarily stepped. One might profitably compare **stanza** sixteen, where Wordsworth speaks of the leech-gatherer as coming to him as if out of a dream, with the Simplon Pass **episode** in Book Sixth of *The Prelude*. About line 600 of that book Wordsworth speaks of an imaginative experience in the following terms:

in such strength Of usurpation, when the light of sense Goes out, but with a flash that has revealed The invisible world, doth greatness make abode, There harbours....

Wordsworth's light of sense seems near to going out at least twice while he is talking to the leech-gatherer. One may also interestingly compare Wordsworth's responses to the vision on Mount Snowdon in Book Fourteenth of *The Prelude* with his experiences while talking to the old Man he met on the moors. He certainly intends for the reader to be impressed with the leech-gatherer's insistence on survival, survival that comes to him, we feel, to great degree because of a sheer act of will. Again, as with many of Wordsworth's solitaries, courage is presented as the capacity to endure. There is a notable difference, however, between the courage of Michael and the courage of the leech-gatherer; nature has not been as generous to the old man who must go on indefinitely from place to place looking for leeches, never being sure he will find them, as she has been to Michael, who, though his farm is eventually lost after his death to owners outside his family, can live the total of his years on land that has been made his own. Michael draws continual sustenance from nature, but the leech-gatherer must draw his sustenance more from his own deep wells of unyielding fortitude. There is an obvious contrast also in this regard between the leech-gatherer and the Old Cumberland Beggar. The leech-gatherer accepts housing from those who will help him, but he does not have the regularity of affection and acts of kindness that the persons in the community of the Old Cumberland Beggar's existence offer to him. Besides, there is again with the Cumberland Beggar an area of nature in which he can live and die, in which he can make his home. Those who care for him are almost neighbors to him. The leech-gatherer is much more thrown on his own resources. It is in this that the poet learns his greatest lesson from him.

PROVIDENCE

There is in the encounter between the poet and the leech-gatherer the work of Providence. Wordsworth seems to say in the poem (and in the letter he wrote about the poem) that this old Man was sent to him for his own rehabilitation. This may seem in some ears to be very close to blaspheming the preciously human, that one human being would be so sacrificed for the instruction and welfare of another. But the rediscovery of stability and hope in the midst of dejection for the poet who writes the poem is certainly the direction of things from the early **stanzas** of the poem, where the glory of the natural surroundings seem to be functioning expressly for the poet's ingesting. The hare that leaps joyfully through the first five **stanzas** of the poem (mentioned three times in the five stanzas, in the second, third, and fifth) becomes in a way emblematic of the poet's life. The hare is also a servant of the benignant Grace of God, bringing to the poet reminders that he is "... such a happy Child of earth. . . ." There may be in the background the Biblical records of God's directly expressed mercy for man, even as incursions that cut with the particularity of biographical facts. But the leech-gatherer comes not so much in the mood and manner of historical encounter as he comes in the form of nature's extension of herself, ministering through an agency that is close to being more a natural agency than a human one.

LANGUAGE

With regard to the language of the poem, Wordsworth is working with a seven-line **stanza** or **rhyme** royal. The longer last line has the effect of slowing down the narrative and giving more time to the reader for consideration. Wordsworth's highly conscious artistry can be seen in his careful use of **similes** that describe the old Man of the poem. The stone and the sea-beast of **stanza** nine, and the cloud in stanza eleven convey a sense of life that is hardly worthy of the word.

On the subject of the language of the poem, one may question whether the **diction** that the poet attributes to the leech-gatherer is "a selection of language really used by men...." In **stanza** fourteen the old Man's speech is described as "Choice words and measured phrase, above the reach / Of ordinary men...."

CHARACTERS

Wordsworth as a narrative poet has most of his characters as active, persons committed to action. He consistently draws his characters so that they are easily recognizable as human beings. They are usually three-dimensional characters that have definite features. For all of his shared identity with nature-which is to a very great degree-we still meet the leech-gatherer as man, not as thing. **Stanzas** ten and eleven are examples of Wordsworth's ability to create character in a relatively few lines; in this he shares a fame that is owned by only a few artists, men like Dante and Chaucer. The leech-gatherer is easily visualized, with his body bent double, "propped, limbs, body, and pale face. / Upon a long grey staff of shaven wood...." Such vivid character-drawing is necessary to give the old Man the action of personality that he has, an action essential to his being for the poet a model of resolution and independence. Fortitude not implemented in action is hardly fortitude. Wordsworth's characters are real because we can think of them as human beings. However heroic the leech-gatherer may be, his heroism does not take him beyond the limits of the human. We have in him no Achilles. His heroism is the kind that can be attained by human beings we know and meet. Generally Wordsworth's characters are real because we can think of them as human beings. The leech-gatherer shares much more with Abraham than with Achilles.

But all of this is not to say that Wordsworth's characterization is simply a matter of straightforward statement or description. Wordsworth's use of **similes** in this poem has already been discussed. As a final comment on the subject, we may notice in **stanza** eleven that rather than storming the beachhead of the reader's attention with utterly direct statement about the age of the man, Wordsworth puts it all in the subtle **simile** of a cloud:

Upon the margin of that moorish flood Motionless as a cloud the old Man stood, That heareth not the loud winds when they call; And moveth all together, if it move at all.

STORY

What about the story in the poem? All narrative poetry to deserve its name must tell a story in one way or another. The story of "Resolution and Independence" has a beginning, a middle, and an end. But it cannot be denied that the story is rather slender. It is more or less lost in the midst of details about natural settings, the feelings of the poet in his state of dejection, poetic figures to describe the leech-gatherer, etc. One may safely say that the story in this poem is to a considerable degree sacrificed for the sake of characterization. The importance of the characterization, the lesser importance of the story, may account for Wordsworth's having written this poem in stanzaic form. Each stanza is really a unit by itself that has a beginning, a middle, and an end. At the end of each **stanza** the poet has to conclude, and at the beginning of each **stanza** he must start anew. Such a structure within **stanzas** would naturally tend to interrupt the flow of the story. The thin thread of the story, nearly lost at times in the larger fabric of the characterization, may be the result of Wordsworth's having an idea-not a story-in mind that he wanted to elaborate in a poem. The narrative structure is there merely to serve the idea, not the other way around. The total impression left on the mind of the reader is that the story is not particularly well-told, but that the idea is indeed well-illustrated. Further, the story of "Resolution and Independence" is obstructed by the poet's insights into himself. The poem is too subjective in character to be a story. The only character that changes in the whole poem is the narrator himself. We are given account of his psychic disturbances, and we are also given the opportunity to observe him moving from dejection to hope. If we are to be engrossed by "Resolution and Independence," it must be for reason other than its engaging story line.

THE MAJOR POETRY

THE SOLITARY REAPER

The poem is about the song that the poet has heard a "solitary Highland Lass" sing. She overflows the vale with her music, "a melancholy strain" that she sings while cutting and binding the grain. The second **stanza** describes the poet's welcome of her song, describes it by way of clarifying that the reaper's song is as sweet as the nightingale's, that her voice is more thrilling than that of the Cuckoo-bird "Breaking the silence of the seas / Among the farthest Hebrides." In **stanza** three the subject of the reaper's song is contemplated. In some of the most memorable poetic lines in the English language, the **theme** of her song is considered as possible "...old, unhappy, far-off things, / And battles long ago," or "... some more humble lay, / Familiar matter of to-day," or "Some natural sorrow, loss, or pain, / That has been, and may be again." The last **stanza** contains the poet's response to the song, beginning appropriately "Whate'er the theme...." The important fact about the music he has heard is that it has so involved his imagination that he thought it eternal, so entranced him that he finds it still echoing in his imagination as he goes on his way.

> Comment

We find many of the Romantics sensitive to music. In reading Wordsworth's "The Solitary Reaper," one may find Shelley's "To a Skylark," or Keat's "Ode to a Nightingale" coming easily to mind. In all three of these poems (as would be true of others that could be cited), the source of the music is alone, so alone that it is either invisible or is very nearly invisible, the area of the poet's hearing is overflowing with sound, the strain is to some extent melancholy, though it might be joyous too. Indeed, one of the abiding characteristics of the poetry of such Romantics as Wordsworth, Coleridge, Shelley, Keats is that the melancholy is at one with the joyous. As Keats puts it in the "Ode on Melancholy," "Ay, in the very temple of delight / Veil'd Melancholy has her sovran shrine. . . ." Further, the Romantics more often than not showed a great deal of interest in the far-away and the long-ago. But the Romantics' interest in that not-present was also more often than not coupled with an intense awareness, a full recognition of the humble and the matter-of-fact. The coupling of these two interests is evident in "The Solitary Reaper." Wordsworth is on the whole more prone to make poetic subject matter out of ordinary, everyday human experience, though he handles such materials in a way that causes them to become uncommon, or romantic. Wordsworth in "The Solitary Reaper" uses such **allusions** as the distant sands of Arabia and "the farthest Hebrides," but they are still fenced in poetically: they are, however distant in miles or tone, within the margin of the field of grain where the singer cuts and binds.

USE OF DETAIL

We know nothing at all about the reaper's real feelings as she sings, just as we do not know what the words of her song say.

In fact, the mystery of her feelings is heightened by the mystery of the song she sings. We might wonder whether she wants to be in the field or not, but we find nothing to tell us, beyond the fact that her song is melancholy; but that does not really say anything definite, for many workers essentially satisfied with their tasks intone plaintive melody. The lack of definitive explanation is deliberate. The poet's intent is to draw the reader into the mystery that he has experienced and has been haunted by. The poem is a success or a failure according to whether we are engaged like the poet in the mystery of the encounter he has had, whether we are made, as he was, "motionless and still." Whatever details we are given (and we get very few details-only in **stanzas** one and four) are to provoke our imaginations so that we will continue the imaginative flow that the poet starts. He only intends to prime the pump. Generally, Romantic art operates not by statement but by suggestion, suggestion through **imagery** and myth. It is not the character-drawing of the reaper that engages us, not in the sense of enumerating characteristics. How much are we actually told about her as a blood-and-bones person? She is alone in the field, she cuts and binds, she sings a melancholy song, she bends over the sickle - that is all we know. But we know more: we know that she is closely allied in our minds with all the associations of nightingale, shady haunts of Arabian deserts, silent seas, far-off Hebrides, old, unhappy things, ancient battles, sorrow, loss, pain. "The Solitary Reaper" is what we create her in our own imaginations to be. The poet will not give details; the reader must do that.

STANZA FORM

The stanzaic form of the poem is an elaboration of the **ballad** stanza. Yet the complexity of the tones and over-tones, the ingenuity of the rhymes, the sweep of the rhythm are not matched by the ballads. "The Solitary Reaper" is a lyrical **ballad** in a strong sense of the term because it combines lyrical feeling and careful artistry with the techniques and relative objectivity of the ballads.

NATURE

As with other solitaries in Wordsworth's poems, the reaper is very nearly merged with the nature that she works within. But, there is also in this poem, as in others, an emerging; the process of merging and the process of emerging seem to go on concurrently. At the end of "The Old Cumberland Beggar," "Lucy Gray," "Michael," "Resolution and Independence," "The Solitary Reaper," we have a remembrance of persons that is very close to being simply a remembrance of the nature that surrounded them; but, we remember also persons as persons, possessing the dignity of human uniqueness, rising above their surroundings, even at times impressing themselves on nature in acts of imaginative assertion.

THE POET'S SEARCH FOR SELF-DEFINITION IN RELATIONSHIP WITH NATURE

Introduction

In one very real and important sense, this chapter could contain with a relatively small number of exceptions all of Wordsworth's poetry to the time of "Ode: Intimations of Immortality from Recollections of Early Childhood." To the time of the writing of that famous poem, nearly all Wordsworth's work concerns his own personal relationship with nature and the values, or lack of values, of that relationship for what it offers the poet in way of self-definition. One may choose the poems of the solitaries for illustration. The solitaries for all of their personal, individual heroism do not exist so much in their own right as they exist for the sake of the poet's, and, consequently, the reader's illumination. The Old Cumberland Beggar is to a great extent William Wordsworth trying to discover the key in which his (and man's) interaction with nature has been pitched. Michael is William Wordsworth too, searching the elements for human meaning, and then for inspiration and solace. The leech-gatherer has found in his near unity with nature a source of resolution and independence that Wordsworth desires for himself; indeed the leech-gatherer moves into the poet's ken with all the mystery and all the swiftness of God's Grace. The poet certainly talks about him as a godsend, as if the old Man had been by the pool ("a pool bare to the eye of heaven") for the express purpose of helping to restore the poet's faith in his own poetic vocation.

Pure Nature

Most of the poems studied in this chapter have an element of pure nature, that is, nature existing in its own glory, in its own right, apart from the demands that the poet's relationship with it make on it, but it should be stressed that it is only an element; it is relationship between poet and nature in each of the poems when considered as wholes. "Tintern Abbey," Wordsworth's great poem about his different stages of relationship with nature, is included in this chapter rather than in the first chapter dealing with poems from the *Lyrical Ballads,* which is where it belongs chronologically, for it is the most enthusiastic, and probably the most complete celebration of the myth of nature.

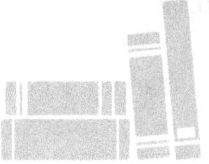

THE MAJOR POETRY

TO THE CUCKOO

This is a famous poem. Wordsworth considered it a favorite. Again it is a poem of complex meanings in the poet's relationship with nature. The poet hails the bird, but then he immediately considers whether the sound that he hears should be attributed to an actual living thing; it may be only "a wandering Voice." The sound of the bird (second **stanza**) is "At once far off, and near." In **stanza** three there is that important word vision, adapted here in adjectival form to describe the kind of message ("tale") the bird brings to him, "a tale / Of visionary hours." The bird's "twofold shout," "From hill to hill," gives the poet as he listens memories of his days as a schoolboy. In one of the most telling of the eight **stanzas** about the bird and its associations in the poet's memory, he identifies it as something beyond the confines of human experience: "Even yet thou art to me / No bird, but an invisible thing, / A voice, a mystery. . . ." **Stanzas** five and six relate how as a youth the poet searched "a thousand ways" for the cuckoo, although he was never able to see it. **Stanza** seven tells that the poet is able as he listens to the bird to live over again the "golden time" of his youth. The last stanza is like **stanza** four an expression of the poet's concept of the cuckoo as transcendental. As the poet listens to the bird he feels again (again is intended to reinforce the fact that this experience is at least half recollection in tranquillity - the present experience is linked to the experience of the poet's hearing the cuckoo in his childhood) that the world of mortals is made eternal. It becomes under the impress of the poet's imaginative interpretation of the cuckoo's shout "An unsubstantial, faery place. . . ." As such, the world is a fitting home for the cuckoo.

Comment

Of course the principal interpretive question about this poem is what exactly is the cuckoo (or its sound) to the poet. The bird as the poet conceives it is obviously not of this world. It may be in the world, but the cuckoo is important to the poet just because it is not bound by the world - perhaps the principal issue of the poem is that the poet realizes that he is bound, and the cuckoo is the agent of his awareness. Observe that the poet calls the cuckoo "wandering Voice," "No bird, but an invisible thing, / A voice, a mystery," that the cuckoo brings the poet visionary revelations, and that it makes of the actual world of facts and time in which the poet lives "An unsubstantial, faery place. . . ." Perhaps when the poet says in the last **stanza** that the cuckoo makes the world a fitting place for the cuckoo to live in, it therefore makes the world unfit for the poet-or reminds him that it is not fit. Readers of the poetry of Percy Bysshe Shelley and John Keats, both included in our critical category of English Romanticism, will, in reading "To the Cuckoo," think of Shelley's poem "To a Skylark," and of Keats's "Ode to a Nightingale."

Wordsworth is saying about the cuckoo very much the same thing that Shelley is saying about the skylark and Keats about the nightingale. Wordsworth is bound by the facts of time, by the facts of a world of concrete natural phenomena, by the terrifying awareness of necessary death. The cuckoo has escaped all of these; so have the skylark and nightingale to Shelley and Keats. But this means of course that Wordsworth is thinking of the cuckoo in other terms than its being a bird, the usual sort of feathery object that one sees perching and flying. He has divested the cuckoo of its physical qualities and has made of it what we would call a symbol; that the cuckoo is not a physical thing is obvious in Wordsworth's calling it "wandering Voice," "invisible thing," "mystery." Besides it makes the world for him unsubstantial. Shelley in the "Skylark" also has the bird unseen, and he thinks of it also as "an unbodied joy. . . ." The cuckoo is for Wordsworth substantive with the world of eternals; it is a messenger of the eternal. Perhaps it is just this fact that shows the poem to operate on two levels. It would be a great over-simplification to assume that the poem is simply a paean of praise to a beautiful thing in nature, a cuckoo bird. We may begin seeing this two-level consciousness in the poem by noticing the yet's in lines fourteen and twenty-five: "Even yet thou are to me"; "And I can listen to thee yet." The poet takes delight in what the bird is to him in the present, but he is at the same time haunted by the remembrance of what it used to be, haunted because whatever the bird is now, it is still not all that it was during the "golden time" of his youth. There is in this sense a yearning in the poem, a pathos for what once has been but now can be no more. The cuckoo remains for the poet a symbol of the eternal, but perhaps this is just the problem: he has come through the grim passage from youth to maturity to the use of symbols, whereas in the "golden time" there was in his lack of consciousness of mortality no need for relating to natural objects and natural creatures as intermediaries. He was, during the time that the present shout of the cuckoo reminds him of, intimately, integrally connected with nature, not only allied with it, but one with it. But this is not possible for him now. He is irrevocably divorced from the eternal because of the adult consciousness of time and time's thousand natural shocks. If the "Intimations Ode" is a poem about growing up, so is "To the Cuckoo," so is a vast amount of Wordsworth's poetry. Whatever the poet's experience of the cuckoo is now, it can never be again that intimate relationship with nature that it was during the days of "aching joys" and "dizzy raptures." "To the Cuckoo" was written during the time that Wordsworth was also writing the "Intimations Ode" (and *The Prelude,* "Book First," and "Book Second"). From a technical point of view, the "Vale, / Of sunshine," the "visionary hours," "That golden time" remind the reader of the light **imagery** of the "Intimations Ode." But with regard to subject matter, in "To the Cuckoo," although the vision is reduced by the adult consciousness of the poet, there is still present to him a vision; the "Intimations Ode" is about a more severe loss of vision.

THE MAJOR POETRY

MY HEART LEAPS UP WHEN I BEHOLD

The concluding three lines of this poem from 26 March 1802, are among the most famous in Wordsworth's work: "The Child is father of the Man; / And I could wish my days to be / Bound each to each by natural piety." It is remarkable how many of Wordsworth's poems deal with the relationship of the child to the world, and, consequently, with the relationship of the adult to the child, and through the child the relationship of the adult to nature. Most simply this poem says that the poet is thrilled when he sees a rainbow; he was thrilled in his youth when he saw one; he will continue to be thrilled by a rainbow when he grows old; if it cannot be so then, he would prefer to be dead. The principal problem in interpreting the poem is probably what line seven means, "The Child is father of the Man...."

Comment

If the reader assumes that Wordsworth has a "message" in the poem, he would probably conclude that the poem tries to teach man to remain as much like the child as he can in the child's purity and simplicity of heart, that he try to retain the vivid imaginative perception of the world that belongs to the child. From this point of view "My Heart Leaps up When I Behold" is close in statement to the "Intimations Ode," for in that poem Wordsworth is saying that he can no longer perceive the world with that peculiar kind of vividness that a dream has, precisely because he is a man and not a child. Obviously in the poem here under discussion, the poet is describing the perception of a natural scene at three stages in his life, (1) when a child, (20) now while an adult, (3) when he becomes an old man. But, after one has read a number of Wordsworth's other poems, one is suspicious of this confident, hopeful kind of affirmation. We may say, "Methinks thou dost protest too much!" The poem, however, may possess its own kind of reserve in that the poet puts his hope this way: "And I *could* wish my days to be. . . ." (italics mine) Does the poet really believe in the exclamation that the poem makes in the first six lines? With regard to the lines about the child being the father of the man, probably the most trustworthy interpretation, trying to read these lines within the context of Wordsworth's other poetry (for example *The Prelude*), is that man's life is significant because there is continuity through the processes of memory. That poetry "is the spontaneous overflow of powerful feelings . . . [taking] its origin from emotion recollected in tranquillity" is, of course, relevant here. But there may be also resentment in the affirmation the poem makes about the child-man relationship. The father may resent the child because the child is closer to the fountainheads of meaning and truth than he, the father, because he is man, can ever be again. This is one side of the confession that the "Intimations Ode" makes. The child finds easily, even carelessly, what the adult has lost forever. The lines from "The Conclusion to Part II" or Coleridge's poem "Christabel" may serve as a gloss on "The Child is father of the Man. . .":

A little child, a limber elf, Singing, dancing to itself, A fairy thing with red round cheeks, That always finds, and never seeks, Makes such a vision to the sight As fills a father's eyes with light. . . .

With regard to the way one sees a rainbow, the worse thing of all is to grow up. The child has far more to teach the adult about seeing the world than the adult could ever have to teach the child-in fact, whatever the adult taught the child would be damaging to the child's vision. That is just what happens when one grows up; one becomes steadily dulled in his way of seeing by the dim world of adults that is constantly being imposed upon him. The "shades of the prison house" that fall in blackness over the growing boy are the shades that adults live in. Perhaps Wordsworth in the seventh line of the poem is expressing resentment that he can never find anymore, however hard he seeks, what was his when a child without having to seek at all. This interpretation would explain the word natural in the last line as effortless, that is, natural in the sense of not being worked at, coming easily with the spontaneity of undiminished vision, coming with the speed and light of revelation. This would mean that each day would be a blessing, that each day would be the most important day of life, that each day, to put it in the terms of Wordsworth's "To a Butterfly," would be as long as twenty days.

But the word natural may have other meanings: (1) perhaps natural faith in the sense of faith in nature, or (2) "natural piety" in that the poet in having the reverence for each day past that pious Aeneas had for his father Anchises would find his life bound together in a sacred unity.

THE MAJOR POETRY

TO THE SMALL CELANDINE

The natural mystery of a flower is not the principal content of the poem. Wordsworth praises the small celandine primarily for its humbleness, but his tribute is not less for its bold, lavish generosity. Out of all the flowers that he thinks of (**stanza** one), the poet takes the celandine as his own. The comparison that he makes in the first **stanza** would identify the fact that the celandine is a humble flower (one editor identifies the celandine as "common pilewort"): "Pansies, lilies, kingcups, daisies," all have great public acclaim to live on; "Primroses will have their glory"; "Long as there are violets, / They will have a place in story...." The first **stanza** very nearly says that the poet takes the celandine as his own because of its humble place in the kingdom of the world's flowers. In **stanza** two the humbleness of the flower becomes identified with the humbleness of the poet: the implication is that he chose the celandine because of his own humble station in life. Because of his discovery of this "Little Flower," he has become as great as the "sage astronomer" who looks up and down the heavens for a new star. He will "make a stir," he says over his find. The boldness and lavishness of the celandine is as remarkable to the poet as its humbleness. But this is just the point about the flower: it is lavish in the way that it gives itself away. Such bold generosity, the poem seems to be saying, is the only real humility

Stanza three reveals that although the poet had met the small celandine many times, he is only now aware of the "Fifty greetings in a day" that he receives from it. **Stanza** four concerns another aspect of the generosity of this flower: with a sense of reckless abandon the celandine comes out with its "glossy breast" before any other creatures have shook off the chill of winter. Stanza four may be the best in the poem, particularly with its splendid **simile** of the "careless Prodigal." If it is not yet evident in the progress of the poem, **stanza** five will identify the fact that these lines on the celandine are written in considerable measure against human vanity, particularly that kind of vanity that requires submission to the values of the crowd. In **stanza** five the "thrifty cottager," the person who lives with the "incidents and situations from common life," the person of "humble and rustic life," is compared to those poets who seek, through following the crowd, wealth and glory in this world. It is the cottager who can rejoice in the appearance of the celandine, not the city-pent, prestige-conscious poet. The poets might woo the celandine, but they would woo it only wantonly, according to the best interests of their ambition. The celandine like the cottager, and like William Wordsworth as he would want to be, finds it good to grow in any place, however lowly the place might be (**stanza** six). Again the poet uses the word careless to identify the celandine's generosity. This **stanza**, stanza six, is probably the most compressed **stanza** in the poem for giving the character of the flower:

Comfort have thou of thy merit, Kindly, unassuming Spirit! Careless of thy neighbourhood, Thou dost show thy pleasant face On the moor, and in the wood, In the land; - there's not a place, Howsoever mean it be, But 'tis good enough for thee.

More criticism of the success-mongers of the world comes through in **stanza** seven. The flowers of "lofty mien" have taken, as men of lofty mien ("worldlings"), praise that really should have been given to the humble celandine. The poem concludes with the poet's promise that he will give "Hymns in praise" of all that the celandine is in the world, and the terms in which he speaks of the flower in **stanza** eight share a great deal with the kind of language in which one hears the Divine celebrated. One may easily compare the rhetoric of the last lines to the language of the Bible: "Prophet of delight and mirth, / ...... / Herald of a mighty band, / Of a joyous train ensuing..."

Comment

This is clearly a remarkable poem. It becomes richer the more one reads it. It is a superb achievement in poetic language. Like the celandine the content of this poem can be found all over the Wordsworthian landscape. In the first place, it is highly penetrating study of humility. The celandine is entitled to fame precisely because it does not seek it. The poem can easily be read as a naturalization of the life of Christ - the celandine is the Christ Who inherits the earth through meekness and lowliness of heart (and the poet seems to say that the celandine unobtrusively preaches precisely what it is), the Christ Who takes no thought of His own safety but throws Himself away for the world He loves, the Christ Who is everywhere in His beauty but unseen until man becomes sensitive enough to behold Him, the Christ Who found His companions among the common man, Who chose His disciples from the lowest strata of society, the Christ Who was born in a stable, the Christ Who was above all things

Prophet of delight and mirth, Ill-requited upon earth; Herald of a mighty band, Of a joyous train ensuing....

One of the most productive readings of the poems one that studies it for its doctrine of the poet (and of poetry). Wordsworth obviously wishes to identify himself with the flower. He would wish to be the "careless Prodigal," who finds his life and the meaning of it because he throws it away, because he takes no thought for the morrow. He would wish for himself the kind of Messianic disregard for security that would enable him to unfold as a blossom on the countryside even while the world were still cold; which is to say that he would as poet wish through throwing away the ambition for wealth and fame, to begin the thaw of a cold world, gripped in the long winter of cold rationalism, formalized poetry, aristocratically-oriented politics. He would be the poet who does not travel with the multitude but takes his subject matter from the lowly, from the common places. "To the Small Celandine" is a proclamation in poetry of the poetic intentions of the poems of the *Lyrical* **Ballads** as Wordsworth stated them in the "Preface" to the 1800 edition. The life of the celandine is full of the "essential passions of the heart...." " The small celandine is the poet Wordsworth wishes to be, the poet who is not the wanton wooer of the standards of worldly success. "To the Small Celandine" is a singularly rich and excellent poem.

"TO THE SAME FLOWER."

This is not as powerful a poem as the first one on the celandine. It operates rhetorically in a similar way, namely in the simplest kind of direct address to the object, the celandine; as in the first poem, the poet keeps his eye steadily on his object, avoiding the second dimension of figurative language. There is personification in both poems, but the power of the simplicity in language is advanced in the obvious paucity of metaphor—there is only one major simile used in each of the two poems: the simile in the first poem is a spear-thrust that gathers into one figure all the separate jabs of meaning, "Like a careless Prodigal ..."; the one principal simile in the second poem sharply cuts the unique character of the celandine by describing another flower, a flower of contrasting character:

Blithe of heart [the celandine], from week to week

Thou dost play at hide-and-seek;

While the patient primrose sits

Like a beggar in the cold... .

Another way of putting the same fact is to say, using the critical terminology of I. A. Richards, that Wordsworth in these two poems is merging *tenor* and *vehicle, tenor* being the subject matter that is illustrated or illuminated by the poetic figure that is the *vehicle.* In the first stanza of "To the Same Flower," Wordsworth expresses the response that was carried by the third stanza of the former poem: the poet's discovery of the celandine was the sweeter because it had been there all the time without his perceiving it. There is in the first stanza also the poet's consideration of himself as inferior to the celandine because that flower is able to live so generously in its humble place in the scheme of things, something that the poet implies he is not able to do. He can only assume that there must have been some time in the flower's past when it received enough praise to live contentedly forever in the universe, however lowly, however insignificant its state might become. Intending to convey an aspect of the physical beauty of the flower, Wordsworth employs the novel reference to the artist who first painted the sun in a design having pointed rays. He says in this second stanza that the sign-board painter no doubt used the celandine for his model. Stanza three is a restating of the content of stanza four of the first celandine poem, but with much less of the dynamic abandon of "To the Small Celandine." Stanza three of "To the Same Flower" has more of the customarily poetic: such lines as "Soon as gentle breezes bring / News of winter's vanishing," and "All about with full-blown flowers, / Thick as sheep in shepherd's fold," cannot rival the raw daring of "Like a careless Prodigal," or the warming contrast of "Telling tales about the sun, / When we've little warmth, or none." The stern humbleness of the celandine is part of the message of stanza three also; the celandine does not fear association with the proudest flowers. In stanza four the poet confesses the degree of his insensitivity: although he has been once too often made lonely by having no companion with whom to share the pleasures of life, yet he has not been perceptive enough to arrest the celandine and make of it a friend. He has been too lacking in vision to find the "bright coronet [crown]" of the celandine, to discover its wisdom made too unobtrusive in its "arch [deceiving] and wily [sly, cunning] ways...." Stanza five is an elongation of the content of the previous stanza and a contrast of the humble celandine to the proud primrose (Wordsworth in stanza one of "To the Small Celandine" had attributed glory to the primrose). Wordsworth uses in this stanza the facts of the celandine's habits that he had explained in the preface to the poem: "...its habit of shutting itself up and opening out according to the degree of light and temperature of the air." The poet has missed meeting the celandine because it plays according to the weather a game of hide-and-seek. But its "arch and wily ways" are a matter of the flower's superior wisdom: the only thing negative that the poet means is that he has missed it —the joke (although it may be too serious a matter to call a joke) is on him: "Thou, a flower of wiser wits, / Slip'st into thy sheltering hold... ." While the celandine exercises its power of wondrous flexibility, the proud primrose must wait for the exact weather that gives it glory: until then it sits "Like a beggar in the cold...." Stanza six is further tribute to the celandine through reference to the fact that the honey bee chooses this humble flower above all the rest, but it is not this time a matter of the physical beauty of the flower. The bee comes to the celandine (being "dim-eyed" he could not know enough of the flower's appearance to come for reasons of its external beauty) through some charm or spell that the flower exercises over it. The last stanza of the poem repeats the statement of stanza two of "To the Small Celandine" but with a different kind of explorer than the "sage astronomer" and with the added "great" of builders of pyramids. There is perhaps also some of the emphasis of stanza five of the first poem with regard to the place of the poet in the world. Wordsworth says that he will be content with the praise of the three or four who will love his poem on the celandine; he does not need the applause coming to the "bold Discoverer" who sails the polar sea, or the fame of the pharoah who seeks to immortalize himself in stone.

Comment

This again is not simply a nature-loving poem, addressed by a nature-lover to nature-lovers. Beware of librarians, particularly the older ones, who say when one checks out books on Wordsworth, "Oh! I love nature, too!" This poem is an indictment of the established standards of fame and fortune although it does not cut with the edge or weight of "To the Small Celandine." Some lines are addressed to those who can only be happy when they add their own particular inane noise to the buzz of "ball-rooms and hot theatres...":

PLEASURES newly found are sweet

When they lie about our feet. ...

With the proudest thou art there,

Mantling in the tiny square.

Thou art not beyond the moon,

But a thing "beneath our shoon"....

Some lines are addressed to poets who are too concerned with grandiose and universal subjects:

All unheard of as thou art,

Thou must needs, I think, have had,

Celandine! and long ago,

Praise of which I nothing know.

Often have I sighed to measure

By myself a lonely pleasure,

Sighed to think I read a book

Only read, perhaps, by me;

Yet I long could overlook

Thy bright coronet and Thee,

And thy arch and wily ways,

And thy store of other praise.

Let the bold Discoverer thrid

In his bark the polar sea;

Rear who will a pyramid;

Praise it is enough for me,

If there be but three or four

Who will love my little Flower.

THE DAISY POEMS

The poems Wordsworth wrote to the daisy, the ones with which we are here concerned, are three in number. The daisy poems, like the poems on the sparrow's nest on the butterfly, on the celandine, on the green linnet, celebrate the occasions of learning humility. These poems are intended to be instructional, instructional to the reader by reporting to him what the poet has learned. The lines from G. Wither, affixed as a preface to the poem, introduce the **theme** of the wisdom at the heart of nature's simplicity. The first five of the lines quoted read,

'Her divine skill taught me this, That from every thing I saw I could some instruction draw, And raise pleasure to the height Through the meanest object's sight.'

In his introductory note to the third of the daisy poems written in 1802, Wordsworth defended his use of the word apostolical to describe the function of the daisy (the third of the poems on the daisy contains the line "Thy function apostolical"). He said,

I have been censured for the last line but one - 'Thy function apostolical' - as being little less than profane. How could it be thought so? The word is adopted with reference to its derivation, implying something sent on a mission; and assuredly this little flower, especially when the subject of verse, may be regarded, in its humble degree, as administering both to moral and spiritual purposes.

These poems on the daisy, as the other poems of the 1807 volumes that speak of small plants and creatures, should be read with Wordsworth's clarification in mind, "as administering both to moral and spiritual purposes."

The flower in question is not the daisy with which we are most familiar. This is the daisy of Chaucer, Shakespeare, and Burns; it is a more humble flower than the daisy with which we augur, "She loves me, she loves me not." This flower seems more fragile than the other kind of daisy; it gives the impression of growing close to the ground for nature's protection; its white or pinkish flower has the quality of courageous tenderness. These impressions should be kept in mind while reading the poems.

"TO THE DAISY."

Stanza one: The poet recalls his youth when he, to use the words of "Tintern Abbey," "like a roe *I* . . . bounded o'er the mountains, by the sides / Of the deep rivers, and the lonely streams, / Wherever nature led. . . ." That was a time when he was "Most pleased when most uneasy. . . ." He refers to the time in his youth when he felt the terror of the beautifully awesome in nature, when there was the delight of fear in his responses to natural sights and sounds. But, the poet says he has come now (lines 5-8) to respond to nature in a different way: he can now respond to the humble, he can satisfy his thirst at every common stream. Stanza two: All the seasons delight in the daisy: Winter takes the daisy to give a touch of beauty to his colorless world; Spring makes the daisy its reason for moving clouds away from the sun; Summer gives the daisy the fields that the daisy owns "by right"; Autumn (like the poet) finds his melancholy tempered by the daisy. Stanza three: The daisy's generous relationship with man is shown in its giving and receiving of greeting; its expansive heart and courage are shown in its gracious acceptance of disregard, and obscure places to grow.

Stanza four: The daisy is less ambitious than the violet and the rose, but it has the reward of the poet's love.

Stanza five: The daisy's ministry to poets offers companionship and dispels melancholy; the poet may discover the daisy at the most unexpected time, for example when he has fled for shelter in a rainstorm or for shade from an April sun. Stanza six: Wordsworth becomes more personal in naming the gifts of instruction and pleasure that the daisy offers; he says he has received the blessings of "apprehension," "steady love," "brief delight," "memory, that had taken flight," "chime of fancy wrong or right," "Or stray invention." The mystery of the gifts is heightened by the use of the word *some* before each of them; that is, by not naming them specifically, he implies his inability to encompass the wealth he has found in his intercourse with this common flower. Stanza seven: The daisy protects the poet from the artificiality and dishonesty of worldly striving. The stanza sets the preciousness of humble pleasure, "homely sympathy," "The common life" against "stately passions." Stanza eight: The poet finds his spirits elevated in the morning hours in the "kindred gladness" that he finds in the daisy's cheerful company; he finds in the end of the day that the picture of the daisy going to its nightly rest gives him relief from his "careful sadness." Stanza nine: The poet has received another gift from the daisy, one that he finds difficulty in identifying: he says it is something like an "instinct," "a blind sense," "a happy, genial influence." Wordsworth probably means those gifts that replace the lost light of imagination that once for him apparelled the whole of creation in "celestial light." The daisy's humble ministry helps him to live with the loss of the "visionary gleam." Stanza ten: The daisy lives through all the year, not withholding its blessings until the precisely right moment of favorable weather. For this generosity it should receive the praise of all men, but it does not. The poet, as if he wishes to encourage the daisy in the continuation of its generous life, prophesies that the future will return the rightful praise to the flower; it is not in vain that the daisy is "Nature's favourite."

Comment

The reader will recognize in this poem many of the emphases of the poems Wordsworth wrote to the celandine. Besides the obvious likeness in the poet's choice of a subject that is not numbered among the aristocrats of flowers—a likeness, that is, in the theme of the nobility of the humble—there are the auxiliary motifs of: the poet's being delighted by the common, his being ministered unto "Through the meanest object's sight"; the kind of generosity that gives of itself recklessly, not planned, not programmed, not picayu-nish; poetry should celebrate the "lowlier pleasure," "The homely sympathy," "The common life"—the poet does not need a new star to write a poem about; the joy that comes in the discovery of the preciousness that one has long obtusely strided past; truth is to be found not with the crowd, but in untrod nooks; the daisy with its bold humbleness runs like a golden thread through the history of creation, serving as a "Prophet of delight and mirth" to future generations.

The student would find it interesting to compare the opening stanza of "To the Daisy" to the lines of "Tintern Abbey" where

Wordsworth describes his feelings toward nature during the different stages of his growth.

Wordsworth seems at times to give a naturalization of the historical revelations of Divine Grace to which Biblical literature gives testimony. It is easy to find this poetic process in the last line of stanza nine. Remembering the Biblical emphasis on the privilege of God to reveal Himself when and where He will ("God moves in a mysterious way His wonders to perform"), observe the "happy, genial influence" that Wordsworth says he received from the daisy in a manner that he could not understand or predict: "A happy, genial influence, / Coming one knows not how, nor whence, / Nor whither going."

THE MAJOR POETRY

TO THE SAME FLOWER

This is a consciously poetic poem in the sense that the poet as he addresses the daisy is experimenting with figurative language. One in reading it easily thinks of Shelley's "To a Skylark," for both poets in praising their subjects exhaust their store of images. But "To the Same Flower" is more consciously, more obviously intended to show the inability of language to capture the grace and glory of the natural object contemplated. The first **stanza** is the poet's affirmation of the worthiness of the subject matter: "For thou art worthy. . . ." The daisy despite its "homely face," despite the fact that it is an "unassuming Common-place / Of nature," has "something of a grace" that love makes for it. The point is that the daisy in its humble glory surpasses any of the qualities that **similes** might attribute to it, whether the **similes** are calculated to advance its essential preciousness through contrast with things of recognized glory or through direct representation of its commonness. Whether the comparison is of the daisy to a queen or of the daisy to a starveling, its value is best known through confronting the daisy face to face. Whether the poet compares the daisy to a nun, a maiden, a queen, a starveling, a Cyclops, a faery, or a star, he ends by rejecting all these "reveries" and goes back to the thing itself;

Bright Flower! for by that name at last, When all my reveries are past, I call thee, and to that cleave fast, Sweet silent creature!

Comment

The interest in the meaner things of nature continues through this second poem to the daisy. It is from these that the poet receives gladness and learns of meekness. The poet says that he is playing with similes, that it is a mere game with him, for he knows that poetic language cannot truly capture and convey the character and value of the "Sweet silent creature" before him. But, of course, though he rejects the validity of the similes, they do each impress an image on the reader's mind. To say that his figurative language has been a failure does not change the impressions of the preceding three **stanzas** (stanza three, four, and five contain the comparisons from which he turns in the last **stanza**). And, too, perhaps it is the case that the suggestion of the last **stanza** causes the reader to return to examine the poet's similes, and then to add his own. It is obvious that Wordsworth in these poems intends to impress a truth (or truths) on the reader's mind.

METAPHOR

With regard to the use of metaphorical devices in the poem, one may wish to observe the way in which contrast works in the third **stanza** to make of the daisy a natural object that encompasses the full scope of nature's qualities. By subtle insinuation this may be an invitation from the poet for man to return to encounter with nature for all he desires in the human experience. The daisy as microcosm has within it the macrocosm of purity ("nun demure of lowly port") and fertility ("sprightly maiden, of Love's court"), riches ("A queen in crown of rubies drest") and poverty ("A starveling in a scanty vest"), the supernatural ("some faery bold / In fight to cover"), and the natural ("And then thou are a pretty star").

THE MAJOR POETRY

TO THE DAISY

This is the third of the daisy poems, beginning "Bright Flower! whose home is everywhere, / Bold in maternal Nature's care. . . ." This may be the most pointed of the daisy poems, not because of content but because of the more compressed, direct language. The other two poems have more expansive suggestion, as if the poet were more insinuating his message than proclaiming it. This poem is like the flower that it describes in its "function apostolical," remembering that the Greek word apostolos means a sending out, a dispatch, a letter. The poet's address is still, of course, to the flower, but he is really addressing man. Rather than offering relaxed situations in which man might be surprised to discover the daisy and enjoy its companionship, the poet asserts the daisy's harmonious relationship with the human community: "Methinks that there abides in thee / Some concord with humanity, / Given to no other flower to see. . . ." Rather than theorizing what might happen to a man who seeks shelter in some spot from rain or sun, the poet states what the daisy can teach man:

And Thou wouldst teach him how to find A shelter under every wind, A hope for times that are unkind And every season?

What takes in the other poems a number of **stanzas** to say, the poet in the one last **stanza** puts pointedly, the daisy's abounding generosity, its lack of pride or caution, its spontaneous willingness, its unfailing preparedness, its abiding flexibility of spirit, its long-suffering love, its heraldic audacity and eloquence.

Comment

It is probably true that Wordsworth uses the word apostolical, for which he said he was censured, with full awareness of its theological connotations. He would certainly know that the word apostle is frequently used in Biblical literature. Although the word has a history in Old Testament religion (Judaism had an office known as apostle), it is found primarily in New Testament literature, where one could easily locate at least fifty occurrences. In the New Testament the word can mean delegate, envoy, messenger, but it is more exactly employed for a group of believers in Jesus of Nazareth, believers who had a special function within the Church, believers who proclaimed the good news of God's redemption of man in Christ. These believers also held particular offices, such as bishops, teachers, and deacons. Of course, those called apostles were highly honored. Wordsworth probably uses the word apostolical with many of these associations in mind. The use of the word peace in the last line of the poem strengthens the probability, for it also has profound meanings within the faith of the New Testament Church: "Thy function apostolical / In peace fulfilling." (italics mine) But again it is important to see how Wordsworth is naturalizing historicity. He does not employ either apostolical or peace with the intention to convey the historical particularity affirmed by Christian theology; indeed the message is that the daisy exemplifies the presence of transcendent meaning within the ordinary cycle of nature. One does not need, the poem says, an eschatological messenger - the daisy works redemption for man through restoring his memory and his reason, through providing "A shelter under every wind, / A hope for times that are unkind...."

Final Note On Wordsworth's Daisy Poems

The poems Wordsworth wrote to the daisy, as those to the other plants and creatures in nature, offer a good example of what is often called, when speaking of romanticism, "back to nature." Wordsworth's poems on the daisy are at once his own attempt, and his invitation to others, to confront the natural world as it is without the help of intermediate steps or measures. Wordsworth's "unmediated vision" is the vision of the poet who pushes aside all dogmas and doctrines, and all incrustations on the purely natural or the purely human. In "To the Same Flower" he says that he wishes to push aside the intermediacy of figurative language and deal with the flower itself.

THE MAJOR POETRY

I WANDERED LONELY AS A CLOUD

One may find it interesting to compare the account of the excursion that Dorothy Wordsworth gives in her Journal on 15 April 1802, with the poem that Wordsworth wrote to commemorate the occasion. She talks of daffodils seen on a walk in the vicinity of Ullswater. Wordsworth reduces the party who saw the daffodils to one: the poem begins with the first person personal pronoun. He tells in the poem the extent of his joy while he was actually among the daffodils, but the wealthier experience seems to have been in the recollection in tranquillity of his association with that "jocund company." It was in lonely wandering that they met the "crowd, / . . . the host, of golden daffodils. . . ." The point of the **simile** of the cloud is not loneliness, but, rather, aloneness. The poet thinks of himself as like the cloud in the sense of being free of movement, free to rejoice in whatever his wanderings granted him; he does not intend the sense of desolation in "lonely as a cloud. . . ." The **simile** may also be intended to suggest the element of surprise in a discovery. The reader may observe in **stanza** two Wordsworth's use of the word danced; he repeats the word in the first line of **stanza** three so as to create the sense of harmonious relationship between the daffodils and the waves that move near them. This harmony is advanced through **stanza** three to include the poet; from line fifteen to the end of the movement becomes increasingly subjective. After stating the gladness of his associations with the daffodils - "A poet could not but be gay" - he moves to a more psychological analysis of what he has experienced; the last **stanza** becomes the most important one in the poem for what it reveals of the poet's own concept of the workings of the imagination:

For oft, when on my couch I lie In vacant or in pensive mood, They flash upon the inward eye Which is the bliss of solitude; And then my heart with pleasure fills, And dances with the daffodils.

Comment

It is easy to read this poem as a practical demonstration of the processes of imaginative creation that leads to poetic production to which Wordsworth gave expression in the 1800 "Preface to the *Lyrical Ballads*." Compare the last **stanza** of the poem, quoted above, with that analysis of "emotion recollected in tranquility":

I have said that poetry is the spontaneous overflow of powerful feelings: it takes its origin from emotion recollected in tranquility: the emotion is contemplated till, by a species of reaction, the tranquility gradually disappears, and an emotion, kindred to that which was before the subject of contemplation, is gradually produced, and does itself actually exist in the mind."

The wealth that the poet received in recollecting the experience with the daffodils was even more valuable than the gold he found when he met them at Ullswater. The alchemical imagination of the poet transforms a lesser substance, the color of the daffodils, into a greater wealth, something like

metaphysical joy. Though the experience of the "outer" eye was joyful, the experience of the "inward eye" was more joyful. In fact, the poem suggests that it was necessary for the poet to withdraw from the actual natural scene of the daffodils by the waves for the inward imaginative eye to work its miracle. The poem is obviously about a poet confronting the phenomena of external nature and the relationship with it that his imagination helps him to discover.

CRITICISM

Coleridge in his critical examination of the poetry of Wordsworth that he made in Chapter XXII of the Biographia Literaria used lines from "I Wandered Lonely as a Cloud" to demonstrate what he considered to be "thoughts and images too great for the subject." This fault Coleridge called "mental bombast"; he distinguished it from verbal bombast. In his discussion of the fifth fault that he found in Wordsworth's work, a "disproportion of thought to the circumstance and occasion," "a fault," Coleridge carefully clarified, "of which none but a man of genius is capable."

THE MAJOR POETRY

TINTERN ABBEY

This poem is written out of the experiences of a walking tour that Wordsworth shared with his sister Dorothy, in June of 1798. The background circumstances are that the two had gone to Bristol to look after the details of publishing the *Lyrical Ballads*. But they did not stay in the city long; they did not finds its buzz and hum at all compatible with their predispositions, so that after about a week they escaped into that country that Wordsworth had enjoyed seeing about five years before with his college friend, Robert Jones. He and Jones had passed this way after Wordsworth returned from his stay in France. The tour lasted about five days. Wordsworth left the following account of the excursion out of which "Tintern Abbey" came: "We crossed the Severn ferry and walked ten miles further to Tintern Abbey, a very beautiful ruin on the Wye. The next morning we walked along the river through Monmouth to Goodrich Castle, there slept, and returned the next day to Tintern, thence to Chepstow, and from Chepstow back again in a boat to Tintern, where we slept, and thence back in a small vessel to Bristol."

The ruin of Tintern Abbey in Monmouthshire had long been celebrated both for its interest to historians and for its physical beauty. Humphrey Davy, a person famous in science during the days we have made the property of the English Romantics, once commented on how much he was moved by the sight of the Abbey by moonlight. But however important the place was to Wordsworth during the tour, the poem itself is not that much concerned with Tintern Abbey - that is, not concerned in the direct sense of being a celebration of a beautiful place in nature. There is in the background of the poem, of course, that whole tradition of the magnificence of the ruins of past times that had characterized the thought and life of the age of sensibility. But whatever there may be of pathos in the poem for the ruined monuments of past times, the heart of feeling in the poem is centered on something else. Tintern Abbey is little more than a pin to locate that terrain along the Wye River that is the setting of the poem. If one says that the poem is about landscape, it is more about the River itself, and the terrain around it. Wordsworth's nature description in its customary particularity is at work in lines 4-22, but the natural scenery is important for what he gets out of it, not for itself. And that is a very important distinction for the student to make when he reads this poem and many others poems by Wordsworth that talk about nature. One may pause for a moment and consider seriously just what Wordsworth means by Nature. For most of the time in "Tintern Abbey," Wordsworth seems to be discussing this natural scene around Tintern Abbey and telling what it has meant to him and what it can in the future be expected to give.

MEANING OF NATURE

But when Wordsworth uses the word Nature, he means more than just rivers, trees, rocks, mountains, crags, lakes, and so on. He means all these things certainly, but more importantly he means a power, a force, a dynamic principle that animates, that molds with plastic might the physical furnishings of the universe. The point then about a man's placing himself closely in touch with rural places and things is that there man comes most intimately in touch with this power, this force, this vivifying and, too, regulating principle of life; the reason is that rural places and things have been the least interfered with by the corrupting ambitions of man. In this connection, it may be well to repeat the emphasis that one finds throughout Wordsworth's poetry (the poetry of other Romantics also): Nature is good, the city is evil. Any reading of "Tintern Abbey" should seek to encompass these greater meanings of Nature. Further, any reading should consider seriously also the human side of the matter: if Nature is to mean anything to man, he must be within himself predisposed in some way to the intercourse. Wordsworth says he is. There is in countless places in Wordsworth's poems an affirmation that Nature and man are exquisitely fitted one to the other. The "presence" that disturbs Wordsworth (in "Tintern Abbey") not only has its dwelling in "the light of setting suns," but it dwells also "in the mind of man."

The discussions of "Tintern Abbey" have in great measure been concerned with what the poem says about Wordsworth's growth from childhood to manhood. In this regard, "Tintern Abbey" has been considered often as a compressed version of *The Prelude* and, too, a very valuable introduction to the "Intimations Ode." Arthur Beatty, author of several studies on Wordsworth, saw in the background of the three stages of growth in "Tintern Abbey" the work of David Hartley, entitled *Observations on Man*, which was published for the first time in 1749. But in a sense, it might produce the more fruitful reading of "Tintern Abbey" to get away from the influence of *The Prelude* on the subject of growth, and think, rather, of three different kinds of encounters that the mind of man may have with nature. By avoiding the idea of growth, one can get beyond looking for connections between the stages, that is, how the poet gets from one stage to the other, and be better able, therefore, to realize the particular characteristics of the encounter in its three different dimensions.

ORIGINS

In view of the fact that "Tintern Abbey" is about what nature can do for man, what nature can give him in way of inspiration and instruction, not only in the midst of the encounter but later as well when man remembers it, the reader may find it interesting to give more than a passing glance to Wordsworth's note on the origins of the poem. He gives this account: "I began it upon leaving Tintern, after crossing the Wye, and concluded it just as I was entering Bristol in the evening, after a ramble of four or five days, with my Sister. Not a line of it was altered, and not any part of it written down till I reached Bristol."

Is this fulfillment of the processes of poetic creation as Wordsworth had talked about them in the 1800 "Preface"? It this "the spontaneous overflow of powerful feelings . . . [that] takes its origin from emotion recollected in tranquillity"? Does the explanation of how Wordsworth wrote "Tintern Abbey" show the contemplation of the emotion "till, by a species of reaction, the tranquillity gradually disappears, and an emotion, kindred to that which was before the subject of contemplation, is gradually produced, and does itself actually exist in the mind"? In one sense, yes, in one sense no. From what the poet says about the composition of the poem, it may seem one of the few works that he wrote on the spur of the moment; he said he started composing it when he arrived in Bristol. But, then, the process of poetic creation can be said to have taken place according to Wordsworth's design as he explained it in the "Preface" in the sense that five years had past since he had been at Tintern Abbey.

FORM

The overall form of address in the poem may not seem to identify it as a poem spoken to Dorothy; but, the final verse paragraph gives the impression that the poet had all the time been speaking to Dorothy, his companion on this second tour of the Wye. On this question, a useful distinction may be made between the subject matter of the poem and the tone of the language that carries the subject matter. It might very well be the case that if Wordsworth had used a form of conversational address throughout, he would not have been able to achieve the high level of seriousness and the dignity that characterize the whole. But in what the poem says-its content-Dorothy is the poet's audience; the subject matter is meant first of all for her. Wordsworth also avoids the perils of informality in a work of such seriousness through using the words to Dorothy as insuppressible exclamations of joy and gratitude.

SUMMARY

Lines 1-22

The poet has returned to the banks of the Wye River after an absence of five years. The period has been longer in emotional terms than it has been as actual calendar time. He views the scene again with all the "beauteous forms" that he has found in his absence to be sources of restoration and inspiration. But, of course, with characteristic discrimination, he chooses only those sounds and sights that serve to put into the reader's mind not just scenery but what one might call the spirit of scenery, or the essence of scenery. The waters that roll "With a soft inland murmur" match the poet's imagination that also rolls from internal "mountain-springs." The cliffs connect earth with sky, but the connection is more internal than the connections of an impressive sight; the poet has "Thoughts of more deep seclusion" than the thought that around him stretches "a wild secluded scene." The smoke that rises from the cottages on the farms around (the "sportive wood" serves as a boundary between fields in this country) stirs in the poet's imagination the vision of wandering people or of a hermit sitting alone in his cave. In the area that his eye gathers in, there is both the wild and the tamed. There are unsubdued cliffs, but there are plots of cultivated ground, measured off by hedges. There is sound, but there is movement in silence. Wordsworth is trying through modifying the nouns with this and these to achieve the sense of immediate meeting between mind and nature. The poet's placement of himself under a "dark sycamore" is not unusual, given the number of sheltered places that Wordsworth uses in his poems for repose and imaginative action.

Lines 23-49

After locating and giving some description of the external physical scene that provides the natural setting for his meditation, Wordsworth at line twenty-three begins to account of what "The beauteous forms" have meant to him during the five years of absence from the Wye and its environs. He has with his internal eye, "that inward eye / Which is the bliss of solitude" often seen these forms that surround him at Tintern Abbey; he has in his absence not been blind to them (Line 25). In the clattering and clamoring of the city, he has received from them (1) "sensations sweet," (2) "tranquil restoration," (3) unidentifiable feelings of pleasure, and (4) a "blessed mood" in which the depressing mystery of life was lightened. The feelings that Wordsworth recalls having had in the five intervening years are emphasized as feelings, not mere thoughts, by his locating them in his blood and heart. The "beauteous forms" of this natural scene around Tintern Abbey were when he saw them five years before actually taken into his being: they were impressed into layers of the poet's being far below the cognitive level-he definitely wants us to know that! Notice the words that are used in these lines to give expression to the remarkable effect that these natural forms have had in the poet's "recollection in tranquillity" during his hours "in lonely rooms, and 'mid the din / Of towns and cities": "sensations," "blood," "heart," "feelings." The profound reaches of the influence of the "beauteous forms" are evident in the fact that when the poet recalled them in his absence, there were emotional associations that he could not identify. They were involved, inseparably tied in, with "acts / Of kindness and of love" that he had performed in his life. That is, the "beauteous forms" had become so deeply impressed into his being when he saw them before that during his absence he did not so much think about them as feel them. And they had become impressed in his being in such a way that they had merged with associations already there, the best associations from the best former experiences in life-kindness and love. It is like saying that objects and sounds in nature were kindness and love concretized; this kindness and love would blend with the feelings of kindness and love already present within the deep folds of the poet's inner being. There is a startling statement in these lines that the reader should not miss; the poet is saying that the sights and sounds around Tintern Abbey have been enough during his absence to show him meaning in life when it otherwise would have been absent. They have provided a "blessed mood" in which all the senseless suffering in life, in which all the absurdity of human striving and disappointment has been made endurable. By "the heavy and the weary weight / Of all this unintelligible world" Wordsworth means all the unanswered questions about human life that leave one with blackness. But there is still more to the blessing they have brought. It is not only a matter of relief from suffering; it is also that the imagination has found in them the necessary materials with which to achieve a penetrating vision "into the life of things." The poet has found in the "beauteous forms" the resources for discovering meaning at the heart of things. Wordsworth is speaking of an active, not a passive experience:

- that serene and blessed mood, In which the affections gently lead us on, - Until, the breath of this corporeal frame And even the motion of our human blood Almost suspended, we are laid asleep In body, and become a living soul: While with an eye made quiet by the power Of harmony, and the deep power of joy, We see into the life of things.

This passage should not be read as a version of the mystic's passive absorption, a state in which all the hindrances of the flesh are left behind through a reduction of human flesh to the most absolute minimum possible. The poet has found a vision "into the life of things" precisely because of the active power of the imagination. The words harmony and joy that Wordsworth uses in line forty-eight are virtually synonyms for imagination. And Wordsworth's concept of imagination is that it is a power from within that exerts itself on the surrounding world. When Wordsworth in these lines speaks of the suspension of "the motion of our human blood," and of the body being laid asleep, it is only as a means to the end of becoming "a living soul." Samuel Taylor Coleridge, close friend and frequent companion of Wordsworth during the time that "Tintern Abbey" was written, often speaks of the imagination in the terms of harmony and joy. Coleridge also thinks of the imagination as an active, shaping power. The "beauteous forms" of the area around Tintern Abbey have provided Wordsworth with the resources for making his life meaningful in times and places when it would have been otherwise meaningless and unbearable.

Lines 50-57

Wordsworth reaffirms the faith expressed in the foregoing lines, with more exact reference to the River Wye. The belief in the power of nature to nourish and sustain through the molding and shaping spirit of the imagination is so remarkable that it may seem "but a vain belief." But he knows on re-examination of his experiences that the belief is a true one. He has in the midst of "darkness and ... the many shapes / Of joyless delight," in the midst of "the fretful stir / Unprofitable, and the fever of the world," turned his inward eye to the "sylvan Wye! ... wanderer thro' the woods...."

Lines 58-65a

But, the poet's return and present experiences at Tintern Abbey are not only the occasion for remembrance; he realizes as he renews his intercourse with the "beauteous forms" and reflects on their ministry to him in years of absence that he is also finding "life and food / For future years." This brings him to consider the levels of his experience with nature throughout his life.

Lines 65b-102a

Some readers of Wordsworth discuss this part of "Tintern Abbey" as a record of the three principal stages of Wordsworth's growth as a poet. As suggested earlier, it may be more productive to read them not in the terms of growth, but, rather, in the terms of three different kinds of experience that Wordsworth has discovered in his encounter with nature, remembering nature not to be just scenery, but the things in nature plus the power and spirit that rolls through them. (1) Childhood: (lines 73 &

74) This was the dimension of experience in which the poet was blended with nature; his movements, "glad animal movements," were the same as nature's movements - there was a unison of life, perhaps resembling most closely the relationship of the fetus to its mother. This is the dimension of experience when there is no differentiation made between the creature and the external natural order than surrounds him. The relationship with nature in this dimension is very nearly osmotic. (2) Adolescence: (lines 66-72; 75-83) The older child begins to be aware of the natural phenomena with which he has been formerly blended. This is the level of experience with nature at which there begins to be a differentiation between sights and sounds. This would have been the kind of experience that Wordsworth would have had during his visit to the Wye in 1793. There is a reveling in nature: Wordsworth uses such telling description as "aching joys" and "dizzy raptures." At this time when nature was "all in all," he "bounded o'er the mountains" "like a roe." The emotional pitch of this level of experience is very high. Wordsworth speaks of it in the terms of a man fleeing from something feared, of being haunted by a passion, of appetite and feeling, of "aching joys" and "dizzy raptures." (3) Early Maturity (lines 84-102a) The adult finds nature to provide "other gifts," which serve as "Abundant recompense" for the level of "thoughtless youth." He comes to find a Divine Presence behind the perishable phenomena of nature. The adult comes to hear "The still, sad music of humanity...," but perhaps it is only for this reason that he can find "A presence that disturbs ... with the joy / Of elevated thoughts...." Only after one has been chastened and subdued with the disappointment and pain of responsibility for oneself and for others is one sensitive to

...something far more deeply interfused, Whose dwelling is the light of setting suns, And the round ocean and the living air, And the blue sky, and in the mind of man: A motion and a spirit, that impels All thinking things, all objects of all thought, And rolls through all things.

Alfred Lord Tennyson, the 19th-century English poet, thought these lines among the finest ever written in the English language, particularly for the way they establish the permanent in the transitory. The passage has been often discussed for what it reveals of Wordsworth's theology.

Lines 102b-111a

The connective therefore indicates a causal relationship between the affirmation that the poet has just made about "A presence that disturbs . . . with the joy / Of elevated thoughts . . ." and the profession that he comes now to make - that he still loves nature, however much his experience in the present time differs from his former experience. In a different way, at a different level but with no less profundity, Wordsworth's love for nature continues; he confirms that he is still

A lover of the meadows and the woods, And mountains; and of all that we behold From this green earth; of all the mighty world Of eye, and ear....

Furthermore, the experience with nature is still an interchange. For whatever diminishing of emotional intensity there has been in the encounter, the poet's relationship with "meadows and . . . woods, / And mountains" is still one of active intercourse, is still one of power and inspiration received and power and inspiration given. The imagination is no less active in this new experience than it was before. The world that the poet loves is the world after the imagination has given it a measure of life and meaning that it would not have if left alone unto itself.

The poet is not now, as he has not been in any experience with nature, a passive receptacle into which is poured sense data from the outside. He receives the "beauteous forms" as "life and food / For future years," but the world of nature that he knows is "all the mighty world / Of eye, and ear, - both what they half create, / And what perceive...." It is very important to recognize that Wordsworth speaks of a receiving and a giving. The imagination is being forcefully imposed on all these natural materials. It is in the poet's intercourse with nature, in his active imaginative interchange, that he finds "The anchor of [his] purest thoughts, the nurse, / The guide, the guardian of [his] heart, and soul / Of all [his] moral being." Unless the "power / Of harmony," "the deep power of joy" were coming from within the poet and meeting the active spirit that rolls through the nature that is external to him, he would not discover the "anchor," "nurse," "guide," "guardian." These gifts come in the active interpersonal relationship, not in a mere passive reception.

Lines 111b-119a

There is through the whole of "Tintern Abbey," and through these particular lines and the ones that follow in this final verse paragraph, the feeling that Wordsworth is discovering truth as he goes, that the poem itself is an exploration of past and present experience rather than any attempt at stating conclusions already drawn from experiences. The exploratory tone can be felt in this final verse paragraph of the poem. Wordsworth turns now to address his "dearest Friend," his sister Dorothy. He hears in her voice echoes of what he was in times past: "in thy voice," he says, "I catch / The language of my former heart. . . ." In her eyes he reads pleasures that were his in years gone by. He asks that he may for a while listen to and see these former times, now renewed for him in his companionship with his sister.

Lines 119b-134a

But Dorothy is not only in the poet's attention (and therefore in the reader's attention) for what she reveals of the experiences of the poet's past life; she is also involved in the poet's future experience, what he prophesies to be the certain blessings of continued intercourse with Nature through coming years. For the heart that loves Nature, for the person who through the strength of imagination creates the necessary conditions for active interchange with the spirit that moves through all things, there will be joy, "quietness and beauty," and "cheerful faith" in the midst of all the "dreary intercourse of daily life. . ." Remembering that Nature is infinitely more to Wordsworth than rural scenery, remembering that Nature is the external forms of things but the Divine Spirit that moves within them as well, one finds the poet verifying here the marriage between the Spirit and the imagination as an unbreakable relationship. Wordsworth attests "that Nature never did betray / The heart that loved her" in language that is very close in tone to certain Biblical affirmations about the faithfulness of God in His relationship with His creation.

The content, of course, in "Tintern Abbey" and in the Bible is radically different, for Wordsworth is not basing the faithfulness of Nature to man on any kind of historical revelation, at least not historical revelation that has the particularity of the ministry of Jesus Christ. The relationship between Nature and man that continued through "Tintern Abbey" has not the definition of a supreme act of revelation once-and-for-all done. The spirit in Nature continues to meet the imagination of man in equally dynamic encounters. What Wordsworth anticipates finding in relationship with Nature in the future is a continuation of what he has found in the past.

Lines 134b-159

One may discover in the closing lines of the poem a fourth level of experience with Nature, a strengthening of relationship with Nature through a strengthening of personal love between Wordsworth and his sister. Wordsworth is through these lines continuing to address Dorothy, but he also, of course, is addressing the reader. He advises,

let the moon Shine on thee in thy solitary walk; And let the misty mountain-winds be free To blow against thee....

With regard to the furnishing of the memory with "beauteous forms," given greater life and meaning through the enlivening, modifying power of imagination, the process that is at the heart of the poet's advice is the same that has informed the poem to this point. The only difference is, as suggested above, that the present interchange between the poet and his sister will make future recollection in tranquillity stronger and richer. In whatever future "solitude, or fear, or pain, or grief" there might be, there will be "healing thoughts / Of tender joy" not only for what the "beauteous forms" of the River Wye are with the force that moves through them, but also for the compounding of these forms and their internal spirit with the present love expressed between two human beings. It is a storing up of the mind with the beauty without and the beauty within and the beauty of the meeting and merging of the two. This is the basis of the poet's trust expressed in the closing lines:

Nor wilt thou then forget That after many wanderings, many years Of absence, these steep woods and lofty cliffs, And this green pastoral landscape, were to me More dear, both for themselves and for thy sake!

Comment

The form of a work of literature cannot in an absolute way be separated from the content of the work. But for the sake of clearer explication and evaluation, critics try to work within this distinction. It may be useful here to attempt this distinction. Although Wordsworth was a rebel against the **conventions** of the poetry of the 18th century, "Tintern Abbey" is written in the tradition of a long meditative poem, a form that had been frequently used by 18th-century writers. The language of "Tintern Abbey" is far from being the language of ordinary conversation, is far from being "a selection of language really used by men." Wordsworth's poetic **diction** in "Tintern Abbey" is skillfully, painstakingly achieved. The words are well-chosen, and he thoughtfully calculates their effect. There is an obvious absence of metaphors and personifications in "Tintern Abbey," for Wordsworth is in this poem following the demands of the "unmediated vision," that is, the poet's confrontation of nature without the intermediate agencies of poetic techniques and language. But this is not to say that "Tintern Abbey" is without easily identified rhetorical techniques.

The poem is written in **blank verse**, which is a verse form that uses unrhymed iambic **pentameter**. Wordsworth's use of this kind of verse form may also be seen to be a part of his reaction against the poetic practices of the 18th-century. A great deal of 18th-century verse was regimented, even stultified, by the heroic **couplet**, that is iambic **pentameter** rhyming in pairs. The great emphasis then was on form, and design, and details were subordinated to these ends. Coleridge had made extensive use of **blank verse** in his Conversation Poems, and he found in it a workable means of expression for the more mysterious, more expansive forms of experience that was the subject matter of his poetry. In this regard it might be worthwhile to recall the fact that 18th-century poetry had also reduced the obscure and the mysterious to a minimum. The more irregular forms of natural scenes were avoided, and the overwhelming preference was for the more manageable forms, forms that could be regulated and confined within the framework of the formal garden. Wordsworth had read Coleridge's poetry, with its highly individualist, highly subjective expression of the mysterious through the medium of blank verse. Wordsworth admired the great flexibility that characterized Coleridge's Conversation Poems; he admired the freedom the form gave for the expression of private meditation on the mysterious encounter that goes on between the spirit in nature and the imagination of the poet. Wordsworth was greatly under the influence of the poetic idiom and verse form of Coleridge's Conversation Poems in the writing of "Tintern Abbey." The language of "Tintern Abbey" has a prose-like quality. The lines that begin the second verse paragraph,

These beauteous forms, Through a long absence, have not been to me, As is a landscape to a blind man's eye...

are too poetic to be truly representative of the whole poem. In fact, apart from the word beauteous, it is difficult to find a "poetic" word in the whole poem, at least "poetic" in the sense that the word was used in Wordsworth's day. One recalls, of course, that Wordsworth wrote in the "Preface" of 1800 that he wished to avoid using the conventional language of poetry. Whatever poetry there is in "Tintern Abbey" comes from some other source than Wordsworth's use of the standardized poetic **diction** of his time.

RHETORICAL TECHNIQUES

One of the rhetorical techniques that Wordsworth employs in "Tintern Abbey" is repetition; the technique has additional force because it is employed in a simple framework. The following lines may serve the purpose of illustration (italics mine):

Five years have past; five summers, with the length Of five long winters! (lines 1 & 2)

These plots of cottage-ground, these orchard-tufts, Which at this season, with their unripe fruits, Are clad in one green hue, and lose themselves 'Mid groves and copses. Once again I see These hedge-rows, hardly hedge-rows.... (lines 11-15)

How oft, in spirit, have I turned to thee, O sylvan Wye! thou wanderer thro' the woods, How often has my spirit turned to thee! (lines 55-57)

thou my dearest Friend, My dear, dear Friend; and in thy voice I catch The language of my former heart, and read My former pleasures in the shooting lights Of thy wild eyes. Oh! yet a little while May I behold in thee what I was once, My dear, dear Sister! (lines 115-121a)

If "Tintern Abbey" had been written in rhymed verse, these repetitions would probably have resulted in monotony (**rhyme** being a kind of repetition). The form of a **blank verse** that is used enabled Wordsworth to exploit a more complex and subtle kind of repetition than that of **rhyme**, a kind of repetition that has its roots in the emotions of the poet.

LEVELS

Further, the conversational or prose-like quality of the language of the poem permitted Wordsworth to operate on several different levels. For an example of the meditative and lyrical levels in the poem, one may observe the way in which the emotional tone of lines 50-57 is set against the more simple and relaxed meditation of line 23-49.

LANGUAGE

One source of poetry in "Tintern Abbey" is the very subtle figurative language that may impress the relaxed reader as being only straightforward expression. For example, in lines 7 & 8 the "steep and lofty cliffs" that the poet beholds "connect / The landscape with the quiet of the sky." At first reading this seems simple enough. But closer examination reveals a wealth of significance in the statement. There is implicit here the characteristically Wordsworthian conception of an active, animated universe. Natural objects connect because there is a force rushing through them, because there is a spirit within them that has both transcendent origins and transcendent strivings. (But in an equally important sense the "steep and lofty cliffs" could not make a connection between "The landscape ... [and] the quiet of the sky" unless the spirit of imagination within the poet were actively impressing itself on the natural scene.) Other examples of figurative language in disguise may be found in (1) lose in line 13, (2) "Felt in the blood" in line 28, (3), "gleams of half-extinguished thought" in line 58, and (4) "Haunted me like a passion" in line 77. This is only a selection; there are other words in the poem that have obliquely metaphoric effect beneath their non-figurative appearance.

WORDSWORTH'S THEOLOGY

The famous passage in "Tintern Abbey" beginning at line ninety-three with "And I have felt / A presence that disturbs me with the joy / Of elevated thoughts" has been much mined for what it could reveal of Wordsworth's theology. Tennyson was satisfied to consider it a grand expression of the presence of the permanent in the changing forms of nature. Coleridge defended the lines (in 1825) against charges of their expressing unchristian attitudes; he found in them the Christian attitude of the omnipresence of God. There is, of course, nothing in opposition to historical Christian doctrine in the statement that God acts through the sights and sounds of nature. The main point of departure from Christian statement would be in confiding the Divine Spirit to nature; the Christian Doctrine of God has always affirmed that God is above creation, acting in it, to be sure, but ultimately controlling it from without. The more exacting theological distinctions would not have been that important to Wordsworth, but he probably would have considered that he was expressing an idea about the presence of the Divine Spirit close to the historical affirmations of the Christian Faith concerning the universal presence of God in the Holy Spirit.

THE FAILURE OF THE MYTH OF NATURE

That nature was living and active, and that there existed the possibility of a marriage between the living Spirit within physical nature and the living, active imagination of man was the faith in the marriage of the Divine Spirit from without and the Divine Spirit within. But Wordsworth, with the stability of character, the granite seriousness of mind, the clarity of sight for the practical and the pragmatic, the sometimes ice water detachment, that characterized his life, dealt with the growing awareness and even translated it into a few fine poems. The first hesitant gropings with life's darker side was expressed as a fertile ambiguity in the "two-level" poems. The virtual acceptance of the darker side found profound and poetically superb expression in the "Immortality Ode." When the fact of the darker side had become anchored fact in his life, there is the more static resignation of "Ode to Duty," "Elegiac Stanzas," and "Laodamia."

But Wordsworth was not so gifted at the writing of tragic poetry as he was at writing the kind of poetry of intercourse between nature and man that made up his Great Decade. His poetry after 1807 was never as great as before. There were only flashes of the old magical inspiration.

THE MAJOR POETRY

ODE: INTIMATIONS OF IMMORTALITY FROM RECOLLECTIONS OF EARLY CHILDHOOD

The prose introduction to this famous poem, perhaps the most famous poem in the Wordsworthian canon, is too long to quote in its entirety. It is one of the notes that Wordsworth gave to Miss Fenwick in his old age about his poetry. The fact that he was commenting on his poetry long after it was written should be borne in mind by the reader; the later Wordsworth was an avowed Anglican who wrote a series of sonnets, "The Ecclesiastical Sonnets," which fit comfortably within the established orthodoxy of the Church. It is probably true that Wordsworth in his later years would tone down some of his earlier statements, statements both direct and implied. Any reader or critic, or even Wordsworth himself, would have difficulty reading the poetry of the Great Decade as an expression of the principal professions of historical Christianity. This is not to say, of course, that the commentary Wordsworth gave on the great Ode is worthless-only that it should be read with certain reservations in mind.

Wordsworth's remarks about Enoch and Elijah have too much of the being-in-church-every-Sunday apologetic about them. It would probably be more true to Wordsworth's mind at the time of the writing of the "Ode" to leave out the references in the note above that have to do with Biblical characters and heaven. The following sentence from the introduction has about it too much of the effort to dust off the Bible before the preacher calls: "I used to brood over the stories of Enoch and Elijah, and almost to persuade myself that, whatever might become of others, I should be translated, in something of the same way, to heaven." This statement as too much the ring of having been stuck in for whatever ecclesiastical ears might be listening. Another helpful correction would be that the difficulty Wordsworth relates having had in his youth over death as something that applied to him did indeed come from "feelings of animal vivacity," not from "the indomitableness of the spirit within him." Whatever immortality that Wordsworth in the "Ode" writes about having been intimated to him has little to do with the immortality promised from the Anglican pulpit.

There is also in the commentary that Wordsworth dictated to Miss Fenwick some reference to the Platonic doctrine of the pre-existence of the soul. Wordsworth on the subject says in part, ". . . when I was impelled to write this poem on the Immortality of the Soul, I took hold of the notion pre-existence as having sufficient foundation in humanity for authorizing me to make for my purpose the best use of it I could as a poet."

Wordsworth did not use the Platonic doctrine of pre-existence because he had a positive belief in its truth, but, rather, because it served well his purposes in writing on the subject of human growth and its necessary consequences.

ORIGIN

The "Ode" was begun in March, 1802, discontinued at the end of the fourth section, and finally completed in March, 1804. In the intervening period Wordsworth wrote the short poem "My Heart Leaps up When I Behold," and "Resolution and Independence." The "timely utterance" of line twenty-three of the "Ode" is one of these two poems. The epigraph of the poem is taken from "My Heart Leaps up When I Behold." Implicit in it is the idea of growth, and of the continuity of man.

FORM

The ode as a poetic form is an elaborate lyric, expressed in language that is both dignified and sincere; its tone is imaginative and intellectual. The ode is usually highly subjective in content, being most often an externalization of the poet's internal feelings. The **stanzas** of an irregular ode, of which Wordsworth's "Ode" is an example, vary in number, length, and tone.

One of the best available introductions to the "Ode" is Lionel Trilling's essay, published in *The Liberal Imagination* and reprinted in a number of places since the time of that book. Nearly everyone agrees with Professor Trilling now that Wordsworth's "Ode" is not about the failure of the poet's poetic powers but, rather, about growing up. As Mr. Trilling shows, the poem is also about "ways of seeing," and about "ways of knowing." The principle of the continuity of the human self is at the very heart of the poem, however great the antithesis might be in the poem between youth and age. Professor Carl R. Woodring has commented on the "organic unity" that one discovers in the "Ode"; he considers the "Ode" to be the very best demonstration of "organic unity" in English poetry.

One may find it helpful to observe the following movements or sections in the poem: (1) The loss of vision (**stanzas** I-IV);

(2) The nature of the loss of vision and an attempt to explain its causes (**stanzas** V-VIII); (3) The reconciliation, the recompense, the acceptance (**stanzas** IX-XI).

SUMMARY

Stanza 1

The setting of the poem is a May morning. What the poet - and he is the one who speaks in the poem-sees and hears around him reminds him of the time when he was able to see all natural phenomena dressed in a heavenly light. However he orients himself in the present, he is not able to see the way he was able in his youth to see: "The things which I have seen I now can see no more."

Stanza Ii

The poet is under no delusion that the change in him is not because the beauty of the external order has changed; he knows that the Rainbow, the Moon, the Waters, the sunshine are lovely, delightful, beautiful, fair, glorious-but he cannot see them the way he was able once to see them. He ends the second **stanza** with the same statement with which he ended the first: "But yet I know, where'er I go, / That there hath past away a glory from the earth." Briefly stated, the poet knows that once he was able see all of creation as alive, dynamic, full of plastic power, glowing with a Divine Spirit within, but now he cannot see this way anymore. A very useful commentary on these first two **stanzas** of the "Ode," and on the whole poem for that matter, is Coleridge's "Dejection: An Ode." Compare particularly stanzas II, III, IV, and V of "Dejection."

Stanza III

The poet goes on hearing with joy in this **stanza**, hearing the birds, hearing the sound of a small drum (tabor), if only metaphorically, but grief comes again. He overcomes his feeling of despair through "A timely utterance," probably another poem-Professor Garrod says "My Heart Leaps up When I Behold," Mr. Trilling says "Resolution and Independence." Then he is able to return to a recognition of the earth as joyous. After he hears the sound of the cataracts, he resolves that he will not impose his own sorrow on the world around him. Realizing the holiday that universal nature is celebrating on every side of him, he asks that the "happy Shepherd-boy" assault him with the joy that exists externally to him so that he might be able to feel, even though he might not be able to see "every common sight" in the "celestial light" that his imagination was once able to bestow.

Stanza IV

Each of the first four **stanzas** of the poem has its joy and its grief. After finding redemption from grief through a "timely utterance," the poet is able to unite himself harmoniously with the spirit of the May: "My heart is at your festival, / My head hath is coronal, / The fulness of your bliss, I feel - I feel it all." The **stanza** sounds ecstatic, and the poet seems resolved that he will not commit the crime of the pathetic fallacy, he will not permit his own internal sullenness to cast a pall over the animated universe that celebrates with such utter vitality; if he cannot see "every common sight" within the halo of an animating imagination, he will at least restrain his gloom-he will not inflict his internal darkness on the external light. But, after a vigorous proclamation of his somewhat stoic resolve, "I hear, I hear, with joy I hear," the awareness of the heavy loss he has suffered falls on him again and oppresses him; he cannot avoid the intrusion of the reality of mortal limits: "... something ... is gone...." One tree that he knows, one field that he has seen are particularly the instruments of leaden fact: "Both of them speak of something that is gone...." (the Tree and the Garden of Eden?) Even so small a thing in nature as a flower announces a tragic change in the way of seeing:

The Pansy at my feet Doth the same tale repeat: Whither is fled the visionary gleam? Where is it now, the glory and the dream?

The "visionary gleam" recalls the "celestial light" with which "every common sight" was apparelled; "the glory and the dream" recalls "The glory and the freshness of a dream." (**Stanza** I).

Comment On Stanzas I-IV

For all of Wordsworth's efforts at full identification with the nature that surrounds him, the first four **stanzas** of the poem reveal the loss of that power that would make full identification possible. The poet recognizes, however passionately he protests against it, the taking away from his sight "the radiance which was once so bright, "the passing of the hour when there was "splendour in the grass," when there was "glory in the flower." The poet is no longer attended by the splendid vision that once was his. These first four **stanzas** not only reveal the loss, but they are full of agonized questioning. The remainder of the poem will attempt to speak with comfort to the loss.

It is probably best to think of the lost power as imagination. Observe the terms with which Wordsworth speaks of what has been lost: "celestial light," "a glory," "the visionary gleam," "the glory and the dream." Wordsworth was writing the first part of the Ode in the last days of March, 1802. Coleridge probably read what Wordsworth had written when the Wordsworths visited with him at Keswick in the early days of April; Coleridge wrote "Dejection: An Ode" on 4 April 1802. These facts make it very useful to read the two poems as glosses on each other. Besides, there is in the background of the composition of both odes all the conversation that the two poets had shared about poetry, what it is and how it comes to be written. But it has by now become obvious that the two odes are about something other than the loss of the power for creating poetry; the poems have been in the past often interpreted as dirges sung by poets who were not poets any longer. They may be about the loss of poetic power, but in the sense of loss of a way of seeing external nature and relating to it, not in the sense of loss of power for writing verse. Both poems are commonly agreed to be excellent poems-strange evidence for the loss of the power of writing poetry! With this clarification in mind, compare the terms that Coleridge uses for the Imagination (he capitalizes the word) in "Dejection: An Ode": "The passion and the life," "A light, a glory, a fair luminous cloud / Enveloping the earth," "A sweet and potent voice, of its own birth, / Of all sweet sounds the life and element," "this strong music," "This light, this glory, this fair luminous mist, / This beautiful and beauty-making power," "Joy," "My shaping spirit of Imagination." Wordsworth in the first four **stanzas** is speaking of a power from within that envelops the earth in "light, . . . glory, . . . fair luminous cloud," and, of course, his loss of it. The essential loss he laments is that he can no longer send forth from himself the "shaping spirit of Imagination," he can no longer command the 'beauty-making power" from within to go forth from him and clothe "every common sight" "in celestial light. . . ." This is not primarily about writing poetry - although writing poetry is involved, for seeing nature and writing about how it is seen are ultimately inseparable - this is about seeing nature poetically. The "Ode" is about vision - and its loss - not about composition. There is in **Stanza** II the sense of a fragmented world, in Coleridge's terms a world that the Imagination has not coadunated. The stanza leaves with us the impression of the disassociation of the poet and nature. Notice that Wordsworth is speaking of light in these four **stanzas** as a quality not inherent in the sights themselves; there is the anticipation here of "the light of common day" in **Stanza** V.

Readers have commented on the forced quality of **Stanzas** III and IV. The poet seems to be trying to make himself joyful, but it does not work. His recurrent sinkings into depression are not that surprising to us, given the disciplined effort he is making toward being joyful.

IMAGERY

The **imagery** in **Stanzas** I and II is mainly pictorial, that is, it is the product of the sense of sight. **Stanza** III on the other hand deals with the sense of hearing. The disassociation of the two senses is itself quite telling, for seeing and hearing are usually combined in Wordsworth's poems. The disassociation reveals the lack of wholeness in the poet's response to external nature. One may feel in **Stanza** IV a striving to bridge the gap.

Stanza V

This is the first of four **stanzas** in which Wordsworth attempts an explanation for the loss of imagination he has suffered. There is at the beginning of this **stanza** the idea (Neoplatonic idea) of birth into human flesh and into a mortal world as a death; the soul of man lived previously in a state of divine perfection. From the "Phaedrus," the "Meno," and the "Phaedo" of Plato comes the idea of the remembrance of the prior state of divine existence.

All four of the **stanzas** in this movement of the poem are concerned with the dismal process of human growth. Wordsworth uses "Soul" and "Star" as the names of that unique power with which the human is born into the prison-house that is the mortal world. There are also "clouds of glory," in which the element of light is again so evident, and there is toward the last of this **stanza** the, juxtaposition of "the vision splendid" with "the light of common day"; again it is best to think of this capacity, this faculty, this gift that belongs to the human self when it is born as the imagination. The first four **stanzas** have shown it to be conceived in the terms of light: before it is dimmed by the thousand natural shocks of mortal limitations, it surrounds all of external nature by radiating outward "celestial light." The human self is closest to its divine origins in its infancy, which, of course, is only logical within the Neoplatonic idea of the pre-existence of the soul in a state of absolute divinity; "Heaven lies about us in our infancy!" The process of growing older is a steady movement away from the fountains of light; each day "The Youth [travels] farther from the east. . . ." For a time he is accompanied by "the vision splendid," the dynamic light-bearing power of imagination, but eventually it dies away, "And [fades] into the light of common day." The "common day" is the life of the adult-Dante at age thirty-five finding himself in the wood. Maturity at this point in the poem seems only degeneration.

Stanza VI

The earth is a prison-house with many shades that fall like heavy, thick cloth over the inner light of the imagination. But the foster-mother, Earth, does all in her power, and with "no unworthy aim," to make the exiled man forget the precincts of light and power in the Eden of Imagination, to "Forget the glories he hath known, / And that imperial palace whence he came." The Pharaoh of mortal time will force the Youth-become-the - "Inmate Man" to make bricks without straw in a parched Egypt, but although the imagination will no longer find God in a lake's surface, the "homely Nurse," Earth, will show man that water is good to drink. The "imperial palace" is most obviously connected with "God, who is our home" in **Stanza** V. It is the heaven of perfection from which "The Soul that rises with us, our life's Star" came. In that palace the "shaping spirit of Imagination" was intimately identified with the shaping Power of God, the I am.

Stanza VII

Wordsworth addresses the six-year-old son of S. T. Coleridge in this **stanza**, beginning "Behold the Child among his new-born blisses. . . ." Hartley Coleridge becomes in this **stanza** and the one following, Representative Man, Man who is still near enough to the "imperial palace" to know "those truths . . . / Which we [adults] are toiling all over lives to find. . . ." Stanza VIII will reveal an important and revealing connection in Wordsworth's mind between the imagination that gives "celestial light" to nature and the philosophic mind. Here in **Stanza** VII we have in strident specificity the steps of degeneration from being "Nature's Priest" to being "Inmate Man," steps that were indeed only adumbrated in **Stanza** V. In a progression that follows very closely the dismal steps of Jaques' speech on the seven ages of man in As You Like It, the "six years' Darling of a pigmy size" (a line bad enough to stunt the Priest's growth) proceeds from his "new-born blisses" to "palsied Age," "As if his whole vocation / Were endless imitation."

Stanza VIII

The address continues to Hartley Coleridge, aged six. The question in this **stanza** is why the youth who still is "Nature's Priest" wishes to hasten his maturity and shrink his immense Soul under the yoke of time-consciousness, under the "earthly freight" of human misery, under the "weight" of routine and habit. In the first line of the poem, Wordsworth points to the smallness of the child's stature as misrepresenting the immensity of the Soul. The Soul in **Stanza** V is identified with the imagination through the adding of the synonym Star which gathers up the images of light in the previous lines of the poem, "celestial light," and "visionary gleam," and which then operates within the context of light in the following lines, "trailing clouds of glory." "He beholds the light," "the vision splendid." The immensity of the imagination makes, in a most revealing connection, the "best Philosopher," and it is the child who, as the Eye of the imagination among the blind of the unimaginative "Inmate Man" reads the eternal deep of philosophic truth. The child as "Seer blest" with the light of imagination burning within is the "Mighty Prophet" who knows **metaphysical** reality. The child is the combination of the Romantic poet of coadunating imagination with the philosophic poet of the Miltonic mold who is at home in moral truth. Consequently, the "shaping spirit" and those truths "Which we [Inmate men imprisoned in the prison-house of mortal limits] are toiling all our lives to find" are naturally, even carelessly the child's possession. The student may wish to compare **Stanza** VIII with "The Conclusion to Part II" of S. T. Coleridge's "Christabel." There Coleridge also addresses himself to Hartley:

A little child, a limber elf, Singing, dancing to itself, A fairy thing with red round cheeks, That always finds, and never seeks, Makes such a vision to the sight As fills a father's eyes with light....

The "little Child" always finds, and never seeks" what the "Inmate Man" always seeks, and never finds.

Comment On Stanzas V-VIII

One may wish to recall that the Alexandrian philosopher Plotinus considers God to be Absolute Beauty and Love and that through the contemplation of Himself, all created things, including man, issue forth. Once the creation that is man separates from God and takes on flesh and blood, he gradually loses his pure spiritual essence. Yet a yearning to go back to God and blend with Him motivates man all through his life. Wordsworth took the Neoplatonic doctrine of pre-existence as filtered through Plotinus' antithesis of divine light and material darkness as a vehicle for treating the process of human maturity and the loss of imaginative seeing and hearing. We should not assume that Wordsworth was committed to the Neoplatonic idea in his own beliefs. He even clarifies himself that he uses the Neoplatonic idea as an hypothesis for poetic purposes. Wordsworth makes some reference, although vague, to the creature's longing to return to a state of divine harmony, but the poem ends with a rejection of the myth. Moreover, Wordsworth's adaptation of the myth is in the most naturalistic of terms. By the time he reaches **Stanza** VII, the language has become so completely naturalistic and human that the myth has lost any of its Neoplatonic mystical qualities. A clear example of the rejection of the Neoplatonic idea can be seen in **Stanza** V. Remembering that light is the traditional symbol of God in Neoplatonic philosophy, we may read the lines in **Stanza** V about the growing Boy beholding the light and its source and seeing it in his joy as a straightforward use of Neoplatonic idea, but then we find the poet casting the last two lines of the **stanza** in such a way that the Neoplatonic myth would have to be rejected: "At length the Man perceives it [the vision splendid] die away, / And fade into the light of common day."

Some critics read the first of **Stanza** V as a consciously intended assault on the tabula rasa epistemology of John Locke. Locke, a British empiricist, denied any innate existence of ideas or moral principles. The human mind at birth is a blank tablet (tabula rasa), and knowledge comes only through human experience. Wordsworth is saying something quite opposite in the beginning of **Stanza** V:

Not in entire forgetfulness, And not in utter nakedness, But trailing clouds of glory do we come From God, who is our home....

Notice the difference between Nature (line 72) and mere Earth (line 77). Earth is Nature with the "celestial light" of the imagination withdrawn.

The word humorous in line 103 has nothing to do, except in possibly a very remote connection, with the modern meaning of the word. It has rather to do with the medieval theory of the four humours.

Stanza IX

Stanza VIII ends in despair; the remaining three stanzas will end in a measure of hopefulness. In the answers that **Stanzas** V-VIII and Stanzas IX-XI give to the questions of **Stanzas** I-IV, there seems only contradiction. Lionel Trilling in his famous essay says that the contradiction must be understood, but that it does not have to be resolved. In fact, he holds that much of the power of the poem comes from the tension. Having explained the loss of the power of imagination, both in its animating, illuminating function and its philosophical relationships ("Mighty Prophet! Seer blest!"), the poet turns to the other sources of human sustenance that exist. If man is to live he must find substitutes for what time and mortal limits have taken away from him. This is the subject of **Stanza** IX-what man turns to for meaning when he has been locked up in the prison-house of mortality, away from the sources of meaning that once were his. The "Shades of the prison-house" have darkened what once was "the fountain-light of all our day," what once was "a master-light of all our seeing...." and have left embers of the eight of imagination, which as the "visionary gleam," as the "vision splendid" apparelled "every common sight" "in celestial light." But the poet professes at the beginning of **Stanza** IX that there remains behind in the embers of the imagination "something that doth live":

O joy! that in our embers Is something that doth live, That nature yet remembers What was so fugitive!

The nature that remembers is not here the natural order (Nature), but the nature of man, his internal being. For the "fugitive" imagination, now fled, the poet (and man) must turn to remembrance of what has been in his past life. When the imagination was a "shaping spirit" in the Youth's present-time, there were continual intimations (announcements, notifications) of immortality; as "Nature's Priest" the Youth found immortality intimated in the "celestial light" with which his imagination apparelled "every common sight" "in celestial light." But the "Inmate Man" must turn to memory-he must look back, not to the present-time-for the intimations to sustain him. **Stanza** IX identifies the sources of memory to be, (1) "Delight and liberty, the simple creed / Of Childhood...," (2) "obstinate questionings / Of sense and outward things," (3) "Fallings from us, vanishings," (4) "Blank misgivings of a Creature / Moving about in worlds not realised," (5) "...those first affections, /

Those shadowy recollections...." Wordsworth says number 1 is the most worthy of human blessings, most deserving of praise and thanksgiving; but, most significantly, it is for numbers 2, 3, 4, and 5 that his thoughts of past years inspire him with "Perpetual benediction." He is saying, then, that it is just the prison-house that he finds to be one of the sources of the intimations of immortality that sustain the creature bereft of "the visionary gleam." Or, more exactly, the creature finds intimations of immortality in his passionate, sensitive rebellion against the prison walls of mortality that have with passing time closed around him. The creature's rebellion is voiced in "obstinate questionings" about the human condition, the facts of the surrounding world and man's reaction to them. The poet, further, raises "The song of thanks and praise" for "Fallings from us, vanishings" - the fallings and vanishings of "the vision splendid": the poet finds intimations of immortality in the falling of the light of imagination and its vanishings "into the light of common day." Finally, among the deprivations for which the poet feels "Perpetual benediction," there are the "Blank misgivings" of the creature man who has lost the "shaping spirit" of imagination and must therefore move in "worlds not realised," areas of creation not brought to their full realization because the imagination can no longer apparel Nature "in celestial light." But the awareness of the loss of imaginative power brings within the poet's circle of blessings named the re-remembrance of the imagination confronting "mortal Nature" and causing it under the impress of "High instincts" to "tremble like a guilty Thing surprised...." This is Nature in the sense of the external natural order, not in the sense of the nature of man. Nature is capitalized one other time in the poem, when the Youth is called "Nature's Priest." The "High instincts" are the innate powers of the human self, the "clouds of glory" that the creature trails as he comes from God Who is his home. The other source of intimations, given above as number 5, are the "first affections" experienced in childhood, "shadowy recollections" of experiences before the human self had become differentiated from the sources on which it was dependent for life. These "affections" and "recollections" intimate immortality in that they "have power to make / Our noisy years seem moments in the being / Of the eternal Silence...." Though the light of the imagination be dimmed and eventually extinguished, these intimations cannot by any event of human weakness or tragedy be utterly abolished or destroyed. Because of these affirmations the poet in line 161 can begin "Hence," hence man is able to know of immortality in the midst of mortality. However oppressed the human creature may become by separation from the far place of home with God, he still may find in those realities for which the poet has given thanks and praise intimations of immortality:

Hence in a season of calm weather Though inland far we be, Our Souls have sight of that immortal sea Which brought us hither, Can in a moment travel thither, And see the Children sport upon the shore, And hear the mighty waters rolling evermore.

Stanza X

Though the time of the imagination's apparelling all of creation "in celestial light" has past forever, the poet says that we will "... find / Strength in what remains behind...." This **stanza** states more directly, more philosophically, what the preceding **stanza** has been giving evidence for. Considering the sources that the poet has found in **Stanza** IX for intimations of immortality, he can begin **Stanza** X with directions to all of Nature to celebrate the season, and we had almost forgotten that the season is May when life is in resurgence! His reason for joining in the celebration is that he has found new strength in the midst of the failure of old strength, he has learned how to live with the loss of imagination, he has learned to discover in "the philosophic mind" resources for continuing life now that "the radiance which was once so bright" has been forever taken from his sight, now that "nothing can bring back the hour / Of splendour in the grass, of glory in the flower...." What will replace the "radiance," the "splendour," the "glory" of the imagination? Wordsworth says (1) "the primal sympathy / Which having been must ever be...," (2) "the soothing thoughts that spring, / Out of human suffering," (3) "the faith that looks through death, / The years that bring the philosophic mind." The "philosophic mind" replaces the transforming light of the imagination.

Stanza XI

It is not by the light of imagination that mature man can live; rather, he must live by the "tenderness, ... joys, and fears" of the human heart. One may find in the use of light in the first and last **stanzas** the two principal ways of seeing the world and the life of man that the poem is written about: the seeing with the imagination so that "every common sight" is "Apparelled in celestial light"; the seeing with the eye of the philosophic mind that gives "sober colouring" to "The Clouds that gather round the setting sun...." The poet says that he still feels in his heart the might of the "Fountains, Meadows, Hills, and Groves," to which the last **stanza** is addressed. But the last **stanza** does not speak of any enlivening, modifying power that the poet exercises over these natural objects; in fact, he is more passive than he is not to their influence: "Yet in my heart of hearts I feel your might...." They do not feel his might, they do not have a glory because of what his imagination does to them. He now lives beneath the "more habitual sway" of the "Fountains, Meadows, Hills, and Groves," and for this he has "relinquished one delight," the delight of seeing them "Apparelled in celestial light." The "vision splendid" has been replaced by the "eye / That hath kept watch o'er man's mortality...." To the poet who has developed "the philosophic mind" as a necessary replacement for the lost "shaping spirit" of imagination, "the meanest flower that blows can give / Thoughts that do often lie too deep for tears." This is not the "best Philosopher," however; whatever triumph there is in seeing "that immortal sea / Which brought us hither," one in finishing the poem still feels that the most precious of all intimations of immortality would be in the "radiance which was once bright," in the "hour / Of splendour in the grass, of glory in the flower...." The "Ode," therefore, may be more about intimations of mortality than of immortality.

Comment On Stanzas IX-XI

Professor Lional Trilling interprets "vanishings" to be the recollection that the child has of the time when he was so intimately connected with his environment as to be one with it. The "visionary gleam" in his interpretation is the perfect union of the human self with the universe. The poem, then, is about the sense of reality that the human creature develops as he grows away from his organic connections with the natural order that surrounds him, away from "the 'oceanic' sensation of 'being at one with the universe'." With regard to the final lines of **Stanza IX**, Mr. Trilling refers to the psychoanalyst Ferenczi's discussion in Thalassa of unconscious racial memories about the ocean as the ultimate source of life.

Harold Bloom takes the "fallings" and "vanishings" to be disruptions of the organic continuity of the human self.

In reading the lines of **Stanza** IX that testify to intimations of immortality from "those first affections, / Those shadowy recollections," the student may wish to compare the following lines from *The Prelude*, Book II:

Blest the infant Babe, (for with my best conjecture I would trace Our Being's earthly progress), blest the Babe, Nursed in his Mother's arms, who sinks to sleep, Rocked on his Mother's breast; who with his soul Drinks in the feelings of his Mother's eye. For him, in one dear Presence, there exists A virtue which irradiates and exalts Objects through widest intercourse of sense.

Not outcast he, bewildered and depressed: Along his infant veins are interfused The gravitation and the filial bond Of nature that connect him with the world. Is there a flower, to which he points with hand Too weak to gather it, already love Drawn from love's purest earthly fount for him Hath beautified that flower; already shades Of pity cast from inward tenderness Do fall around him upon aught that bears Unsightly marks of violence or harm. Emphatically such a Being lives. Frail creature as he is, helpless as frail, An inmate of this active universe: For feeling has to him imparted power That through the growing faculties of sense, Doth like an agent of the one great Mind Create, creator and receiver both. Working but in alliance with the works Which it beholds. - Such, verily, is the first Poetic spirit of our human life, By uniform control of after years, In most, abated or suppressed; in some, Through every change of growth and of decay Pre-eminent till death.

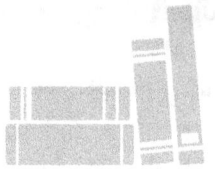

THE MAJOR POETRY

WHAT CRITICS HAVE THOUGHT OF THE WORK OF WILLIAM WORDSWORTH

Literary history is the story of the ebb and flow of different sensibilities. The ingenious conceits of the **metaphysical** poets, for example, were replaced by the majestic march of the heroic **couplet**. The military regularity of the heroic **couplet** (see the poetry of Alexander Pope) was, for another example, replaced by the fluidity of the **blank verse** of Samuel Taylor Coleridge's Conversation Poems, and by the multifarious lyrical inventiveness of Percy Bysshe Shelley.

The Romantic Movement in English Literature was largely an attempt to find new modes of expression for the sensibility that developed in the last decades of the 18th century. Wordsworth was himself aware that he was representing a new sensibility, one that did not have a critical tradition to support it. Therefore he found himself obliged to publish the *Lyrical Ballads* "as an experiment." The famous "Preface to the *Lyrical Ballads*," 1800 edition, was quite deliberately presented as an explanation of the departures his poetry made from the customary poetic practices of the times; in it he defended both the theoretical basis of his poetry and the ways in which he had put theory into actual practice. But it was not only at the beginning of his career that he found it necessary to be an apologist for his work; it was necessary to do so, he felt, through his life. He was misunderstood and disliked by many, but gradually through the years he was given a place in English letters commensurate with his endowments and achievements.

Samuel Taylor Coleridge, poet and critic, was one of the earliest persons to give recognition to the quality of Wordsworth's work and to give the poet self-confidence. Coleridge's critical work, Biographia Literaria, reflects the degree of its author's enthusiasm about the poetry of Wordsworth. References to Wordsworth are rife in the Biographia, but most of what Coleridge has to say about Wordsworth is in chapters XIV, XVII, XVIII, and XXII.

HAZLITT

William Hazlitt, another contemporary of Wordsworth, showed a great deal of interest in Wordsworth's work. His criticisms of Wordsworth range from the highly subjective, though extremely significant memoirs (*My First Acquaintance with Poets*) to highly perceptive criticisms (*The Spirit of the Age*). For some time Hazlitt was revolted by what he thought to be political heresy in Wordsworth's writings. Later he changed his evaluation and tried to make amends for the abusive criticism he had leveled at Wordsworth's work. If Hazlitt at one time considered The Excursion the most effective example of Wordsworth's egocentricity and his total deficiency "in all the machinery of poetry," he later said that Wordsworth's poetry was distinguished by "a proud humility."

KEATS

John Keats, one of the Second Generation of English Romantic poets, almost worshipped Wordsworth at the outset of his literary career. He said of him in a **sonnet** of 19 November 1816, Great spirits now on earth are sojourning; He of the cloud, the cataract, the lake, Who on Helvellyn's summit, wide awake, Catches his freshness from Archangel's wing....

But Keats's attitudes toward Wordsworth were not always so complimentary; in fact he wavered a great deal in what he said of Wordsworth.

Thomas DeQuincey, another English Romantic, knew Wordsworth personally. DeQuincey considered Wordsworth's theories about poetic **diction** to have worked seriously against his popularity.

WORDSWORTHIAN CRITICISM IN THE VICTORIAN AGE

In a true sense the Victorian era in literature can be safely termed "romantic." The critical theory of the Victorians took for granted the assumptions of the Romantic critics. Consequently, Wordsworth's reputation reached a very high mark of popularity in the Victorian Period. Walter Pater in his popular Appreciations speaks of Wordsworth's sincerity, his sense of the presence of being and life in inanimate natural objects, his penetration through the exterior of things to the quintessential, and his sense of continuity.

STEPHEN

Another eminent Victorian figure, Leslie Stephen, set forth the idea that Wordsworth was not merely a lyric poet but also a philosopher, even a systematic one. Stephen said that Wordsworth in his work tried to provide the answers to principal **metaphysical** questions. The basis of Wordsworth's system, according to Stephen, is the continuity established between the child's instincts and the mature man's reason.

ARNOLD

Leslie Stephen's essay provoked a reply from Matthew Arnold, the best-known of the Victorian critics. Arnold edited a selection of Wordsworth's poetry and wrote an introduction to it. He refused to accept Leslie Stephen's attempt to make a systematic philosopher of Wordsworth, and said, rather, that Wordsworth's best poems were the shorter ones, not the ponderously philosophical poems such as *The Prelude* and *The Excursion*.

WORDSWORTHIAN CRITICISM IN OUR TIMES

Readers and critics in our times are showing a great deal of interest in and sympathy for the Romantics; Wordsworth is generally agreed to be the greatest of the Romantics. The early decades of our century were pretty clearly anti-Romantic, probably because of the oversimplifications committed by Victorian critics in their readings of the Romantics.

CRITICISMS

T. E. Hulme in an essay on classicism and romanticism, written before the First World War, frankly stated his objection to the best of the Romantics. T. S. Eliot, one of the famous persons in contemporary Western Literature, has been condescending toward the Romantics. The strongest opponents of the Romantics are the New Humanists. In *Shelburne Essays, Seventh Series* (1910), Paul Elmer More devoted an essay to Wordsworth in which he showed disapproval not only of the poet Wordsworth but of the man Wordsworth as well. He considered him lacking in "native vitality," and he considered the philosophical basis of his poetry to be sentimental and weak. Irving Babbitt wrote even more disparagingly of Wordsworth's poetry. There is a chapter titled "The Primitivism of Wordsworth" in Babbitt's *On Being Creative;* in that chapter Babbitt attacks Wordsworth's "wise passiveness" as a kind of surrender of the human reason to base instincts.

A. L. Huxley as violently as any of the Humanists attacked Wordsworth. In an article first published in 1929, "Wordsworth in the Tropics," Huxley accused Wordsworth as lacking in any real sense of tragedy and as having no awareness of the ruthlessness of natural forces. Huxley argues that Wordsworth's vision would have been entirely different if he had been reared in the tropics.

THE NEW CRITICS

Another kind of indictment came from the New Critics, who assumed a critical position that argues for the autonomy of a poem, that finds no need to interpret in the context of other spheres of human activity. Showing a preference for paradox,

irony, and elaborate metaphors, the metaphysical poetry of the 17th century and the poetry of wit of the 18th century are their favorites. William Empson in *Seven Types of Ambiguity* (1930) considered the Romantics as mere escapists. He rejected "Tintern Abbey" for want of paradox and ambiguity. Although Cleanth Brooks showed a greater sympathy in *The Well-Wrought Urn* for Wordsworth's "Immortality Ode" than is customary among the New Critics, he considered the poem to fail at the end in the dramatization of its arguments.

A NEW REGARD

After the Second World War, a trend began toward the rehabilitation of regard for the Romantics. Wordsworth since that time has been greatly lauded. J. W. Beach in an article titled "Reason and Nature in Wordsworth" (*Journal of the History of Ideas*, 1940) replies to the charges of Babbitt, More, et. al. that Wordsworth had placed instinct above reason and had confused the ethical with the merely natural. Richard H. Fogle in two studies ("Romantic Bards and **Metaphysical** Reviewers" (1945); "A Recent Attack upon Romanticism" (1948)) defended the Romantics (including Wordsworth) against the attacks of the New Critics.

A very recent study of Wordsworth by Carl R. Woodring is a good place for any student to begin his acquaintance with past and present opinion on the poet. The unusual value of Woodring's book is that he presupposes hundreds of previous studies of Wordsworth and further offers many new insights into the poems. There is an intelligent balance between what other readers of Wordsworth have said and what needs to be said in the present. As with Professor Woodring's other critical studies (see particularly *Politics in the Poetry of Coleridge*), the student can be certain that he is getting a reading of poems within the context of accurate, relevant historical material. And this kind of reading is not as easily come by as one might suppose! The book is titled Wordsworth and is published in paperback by Houghton Mifflin Company as one in a series of "Riverside Studies in Literature."

THE MAJOR POETRY

ESSAY QUESTIONS AND ANSWERS

Question: What is Wordsworth's attitude toward Nature?

Answer: The popular conception of his attitude to nature is that of a simple-minded contemplation of "nature's holy plan." But this generalization will never do. There is, in fact, a range of attitudes toward nature expressed in Wordsworth's poems. In some places he praises natural scenery for its external beauty; in many-probably most-places he stands in awe of the Divine Spirit that rolls through the created order, giving it life, form, even personality; in some places Wordsworth expresses great antagonism toward nature, recognizing in it the dimension of the immutable that is unavailable to time-bound creatures like man. There may even be great ambiguity of attitude in a single poem: the poet may praise natural sights and sounds for their own physical loveliness, he may see through the external and find his imagination married with the Divine Spirit within, he may express a level of resentment at the limitation on his vision. It is close to absolute fact to say that Wordsworth stresses the conception of an animated cosmos; in this way he is a reactionary against the mechanistic view of the universe held by his predecessors.

It may be possible to abstract the four following positions from his works:

(1) The poet feels that all his creative force is simply and merely the product of nature's influences. All that man is required to do is surrender to the forces of nature in "wise passiveness."

(2) The poet denies the validity of natural forces. The imagination is the source of creative energy, and unless the "shaping spirit of Imagination" is brought to bear on natural surroundings, they remain dead, fixed objects.

(3) The third attitude is the most pervasive in Wordsworth's poetry. It is a middle attitude between the former two, or, perhaps, better, it is a combination of the former two attitudes. There is an interchange between the imagination of man and nature, a meeting, sometimes a merging, more often an interpersonal relationship. Readers of Wordsworth frequently discuss his materpieces in terms of the Thy Myth of the Great Marriage.

(4) The sudden death of Wordsworth's brother John was the beginning of a turn in his conception of the nature-man relationship; the subsequent tragedies that he suffered made the turn one of more severity. Wordsworth became aware of the hostility of the created order toward the welfare of man, that man is set in the midst of physical forces that make him a creature of sorrow and death. The sea was no longer just a sea but an instrument of destruction. The marriage between the imagination and man becomes impossible because man is mortal, and nature is eternal. At least one dissertation has been written on the English Romantics as forerunners of modern

existentialists; this change in Wordsworth's attitude may serve to illustrate the reason for such a thesis.

Question: Discuss Wordsworth's achievement as a narrative poet.

Answer: Trying to revitalize poetry along the lines reviewed in the 1800 "Preface to the *Lyrical Ballads,*" Wordsworth found that the narrative form was almost entirely neglected by 18th-century poets; he felt that it had a rich potential, and he did not hesitate to exploit it.

o The very title of the first volume of his poetry, *Lyrical Ballads,* points to his interest in the narrative **genre**. Wordsworth was to show great skill in manipulating the techniques of the narrative form. The characters in Wordsworth's narrative poems are quite active and have definite personalities. Michael is certainly a three-dimensional figure, who, for all his existence as William Wordsworth-projected, has the mind and spirit of a real human being. The leech-gatherer of "Resolution and Independence," for all his heroism, is a human being grown old. One could find him easily on a park bench, or slowly moving in bent posture along a country road.

Wordsworth's narrative poems in most cases try to teach a lesson. Sometimes the teaching is too much preachment, as is "The Old Cumberland Beggar." In "Michael," agreed by nearly all to be a masterpiece, the moral is interwoven into the texture of the poem, so that it meets one quietly and naturally, not in loud tones from a pulpit. We participate in an ethical metamorphosis when reading "Michael," without being aware of it.

There are some poems by Wordsworth that are narrative, but in a much less obvious sense than the term narrative usually implies. The exquisite Lucky Poems, "Lucy Gray," and "The Reverie of Poor Susan" are all narrative poems, but they hardly tell a story. The partial disappearance of the story in these poems may be attributed to the fact that in them Wordsworth is concerned more with psychological than with external actions. Consequently, our concern in reading the *Lucy Poems* is more with the drama of the poet's inner self-his awakening to the grim reality death - than with any kind of external action.

Question: Why can we call Wordsworth the poet of the democratic idea?

Answer: In "Preface to the *Lyrical Ballads,*" 1800, the most important single document to read for a straightforward presentation of Wordsworth's poetic credo, he declared that he had for his poems proposed "to choose incidents and situations from common life, and to relate or describe them, throughout, as far as was possible in a selection of language really used by men...." All through this literary manifesto the cause of the common man is embraced and extolled. Wordsworth carried out his intention with faithfulness, at least in the choice of figures that he made. His poems are about such humble characters as Lucy Gray, the Old Cumberland Beggar, and Poor Susan; other representative figures can easily be found. When such humble characters as these figured in the literature of Wordsworth's predecessors, they were usually the easy target of ridicule. Wordsworth goes to the opposite extreme of endowing them with the attributes of heroes.

Wordsworth's method is basically an attempt to strip off the non-human, both in life and in art. What we are left with is not the human being of rank and degree, but the human being with all his dignity and with all his pitfalls. The basic principal of the democratic philosophy of government is that each man is as good and deserving as the next man, and every citizen has a right to vote. Wordsworth was a moral philosopher in this sense: he tried to create in man's heart respect for the human individual for what he is, not for the wealth and fame that he might come to possess.

Question: What are some of the principal ways in which the "Immortality Ode" is important in the Wordsworthian canon?

Answer: The passage from innocence to experience is, in Romantic poetry, a recurrent motif. All Romantic poets wrote a series of poems on this theme. The "Immortality Ode" belongs to the innocence-to-experience poetry of the Romantic Period.

In his early poetry Wordsworth celebrated the marriage between nature and his own imagination. We may speak of this union as innocence, for the poet experiences a deep sense of security. But the passage to experience occurs in the realization that the sense of security was a false one. With the poet's new awareness of death, the union between nature and the imagination in replaced by a sense of separateness and isolation, both characteristics of the stage of experience in human life. Many critics say that the "Immortality Ode" was written exactly as this moment of spiritual crisis in the poet's life. The poem certainly marks a turning point in the history of his work. Gone was the passionate exuberance with which Wordsworth felt his imagination married to nature; gone too were the great poems celebrating the marriage. The poet's eye had come to keep watch over man's mortality.

Wordsworth made an heroic effort to deal with the loss of "the visionary gleam." In the final **stanza** of the "Intimations Ode," he hinted that the kind of poetry he would be writing from this point would be tragic poetry, but many critics claim that

Wordsworth never kept his promise because his poetic genius was not equipped for the creation of that kind of verse. One may find reason to differ with such statements, but it can hardly be denied that the poetry Wordsworth composed after the "Immortality Ode" fell far short of the greatness of the poetry of the Great Decade, 1797 to 1807.

Question: What are some of the principal characteristics of Wordsworth's style?

Answer: An illustration from a poem may be the best beginning for an answer to this question. In "To the Same Flower" (following "To the Daisy" of 1802), Wordsworth says he plays with **similes** so as to find a fitting figure of speech for expressing his feelings about the daisy. In the final **stanza** he confesses his failure:

Bright Flower! for by that name at last, When all my reveries are past, I call thee, and to that cleave fast, Sweet silent creature! That breath'st with me in sun and air, Do thou, as thou art wont, repair My heart with gladness, and a share Of thy meek nature!

These lines are expressing the poet's rejection of any kind of figurative language; he decides that it is necessary for him to move through the intermediate means of **metaphor** and get back to the object itself. Wordsworth believed that the most poetic of all worlds was the real world, naked of poetic **imagery**. This conviction led him to leave behind the metaphoric tinsel and neon phraseology of his contemporary writers. That unpretentious, unostentatious, even ascetic quality that a reader finds in so much of Wordsworth's poetry is the result of Wordsworth's attitudes toward tenor and vehicle. Matthew Arnold spoke of Wordsworth's poetry as being bare and grand like a mountain top. The *Lucy Poems*, among the most frequently read of Wordsworth's verse, show the poet's belief that the merely literal statement of the human condition is quite adequate; there is no need to decorate the truth with fancy metaphoric dress and figurative trappings. Take, for example, the following lines from "A Slumber Did My Spirit Seal":

No motion has she now, no force; She neither hears nor sees; Rolled round in earth's diurnal course, With rocks, and stones, and trees.

But, it should be noted by any reader that the effects Wordsworth achieves in his poetry are not generally the result of his employing in his poems "a selection of language really used by men. . . ." On the contrary the effects of Wordsworth's poetry are the fruit of studied efforts on the poet's part to find the exact word for what he is trying to express.

Question: In what ways did Wordsworth widen the scope of English Poetry?

Answer: Wordsworth felt that he was revolutionizing English poetry. We can say that he was entitled to those feelings, for English poetry followed a very different course after his time. New areas and facets of human experience, formerly unexplored by poets, were now made the subject matter of poetry. Although the following five statements oversimplify the ambiguity of some of his efforts, they do serve as workable generalizations:

(1) Wordsworth proved that the lower strata of society is a fit subject for poetry.

(2) Wordsworth stressed the importance of human emotion and spontaneity, and by so doing liberated English poetry from the closely confining intellectualism and false sophistication of Neoclassical poetry.

(3) Wordsworth introduced the **ballad** form into a new importance in English poetry.

(4) Wordsworth reinstated simplicity as a criterion for the evaluation of the merits of poetry.

(5) Wordsworth was revolutionary in writing poetry that he intended to be considered as an experiment.

BIBLIOGRAPHY

EDITIONS OF THE POET'S WORK

The Poetical Works of William Wordsworth, ed. Ernest de Selincourt and Helen Darbishire. Five volumes. Oxford: Clarendon, 1940-49. Miss Darbishire issued a Second Edition of Volumes I-III in 1952-54.

The Prelude, or Growth of a Poet's Mind, ed. Ernest de Selincourt. Second Edition, revised by Helen Darbishire. Oxford: Clarendon. 1959. This is the sixth volume of Poetical Works.

The Prose Works of William Wordsworth, ed. Alexander B. Grosart. Three volumes. London: Moxon, 1876. This is a superior edition to that of William Knight.

The Early Letters of William and Dorothy Wordsworth (1787-1805), ed. Ernest de Selincourt. Oxford: Clarendon, 1935. Chester L. Shaver is doing a revision.

The Letters of William and Dorothy Wordsworth: The Middle Years, ed Ernest de Selincourt. Two volumes. Oxford: Clarendon, 1937.

The Letters of William and Dorothy Wordsworth: The Later Years, ed. Ernest de Selincourt. Three volumes. Oxford: Clarendon, 1939.

The Correspondence of Henry Crabb Robinson with the Wordsworth Circle (1808-1866), ed. Edith J. Morley. Two volumes. Oxford: Clarendon, 1927.

Some Letters of the Wordsworth Family ..., ed. Leslie N. Broughton. Ithaca: Cornell, 1942. Cornell Studies in English, Vol. 32.

Wordsworth and Reed: The Poet's Correspondence With His American Editor, 1836-1850, ed. Leslie N. Broughton. Ithaca: Cornell, 1933. Cornell Studies in English, Vol. 21.

BIOGRAPHICAL STUDIES

De Selincourt, Ernest. *Dorothy Wordsworth: A Biography.* Oxford: Clarendon, 1933. Of the several available works on William Wordsworth's sister, this is the most comprehensive. It is useful to read this work as a companion volume to Dorothy Wordsworth's letters.

Harper, George McLean. *William Wordsworth: His Life, Works, and Influence.* Third Edition. New York: Scribner's, 1929. This has been the standard biography. It will be replaced by Mrs. Moorman's work when it is finished.

Legouis, Emile. *The Early Life of William Wordsworth,* 1770-1798: A Study of *The Prelude,* trans. J. W. Matthews. New York: Dutton (1932). This biography has a good reputation for historical criticism. Thorough.

Meyer, George Wilbur. *Wordsworth's Formative Years.* Ann Arbor: Michigan, 1943. University of Michigan Publications in Language and Literature, No. 20. The distinctive trait of this work is that it employs sources other than *The Prelude* to study the early life of Wordsworth.

Moorman, Mary. *William Wordsworth: A Biography. The Early Years, 1770-1803.* Oxford: Clarendon, 1957. This is the most thorough biography of

Wordsworth written to the present time. There will be a continuation of the work in other volumes.

Wordsworth, Christopher. *Memoirs of William Wordsworth, Poet-Laureate, D.C.L.* Two volumes. London: Moxon, 1851. Written from the point of view of family involvements by Wordsworth's nephew. It uses family papers, family relationships, and reveals the seamier side of family loyalty and disloyalty.

CRITICISM OF THE POET'S WORKS

Abrams, M. H. *The Mirror and the Lamp: Romantic Theory and the Critical Tradition.* New York: W. W. Norton and Company, Inc., 1958. A most remarkable book on the history of criticism. The parts that deal with Wordsworth's criticism (especially Chapter V) are among the best on the subject-perhaps the best.

Bannerjee, Srikumar. *Critical Theories and Poetic Practice in the* Lyrical Ballads. London: Williams and Norgate, 1931. This book has the advantage for the student of pulling a great deal together in one place.

Bateson, F. W. *Wordsworth: A Re-interpretation.* London: Longmans, 1954. This book has a very good reputation except for what is generally agreed to be an excessive emphasis on Wordsworth's incestuous love for his sister.

Batho, Edith C. *The Later Wordsworth.* Cambridge University Press, 1933; reprinted, New York: Russell and Russell, 1963. A study of William Wordsworth as conservative. A good book for reading with "The Ecclesiastical Sonnets."

Beatty, Arthur. *William Wordsworth: His Doctrine and Art in Their Historical Relations.* Second Edition. Madison: Wisconsin, 1927. University of

Wisconsin Studies in Language and Literature, No. 24. David Hartley's influence on Wordsworth is the main concern here.

Bloom, Harold. *The Visionary Company.* New York: Doubleday and Company, Inc., 1963. A highly suggestive reading of Wordsworth, using more the psychological approach than the historical. Professor Bloom wishes to read poems by the English Romantics from a Blakean point of view. Provocative, but in some ways misleading. Should be read with reservations and with the idea that it is not the only book on Wordsworth that one encounters.

Bostetter, Edward E. *The Romantic Ventriloquists: Wordsworth, Coleridge, Keats, Shelley, Byron.* Seattle: Washington, 1963. Readings of the English Romantics as being trapped by their own visions. Only Byron found the way out, through laughing at himself, at the world, at God, at everything. An existentialist reading of Wordsworth.

Bowra, C. M. *The Romantic Imagination.* New York: Oxford University Press, 1961. Chapter Four is a close reading of the "Immortality Ode." Sane.

Brinton, C. *The Political Ideas of the English Romanticists.* Oxford: Oxford University Press, 1963. A chapter on Wordsworth deals with his early revolutionary ideas and the later more conservative man.

Brooke, Stopford A. *Theology in the English Poets: Cowper-Coleridge-Wordsworth-and Burns.* London: Kegan Paul, 1874. The movement of ideas in *The Prelude.* Generally agreed to be reliable.

Burton, Mary E. *The One Wordsworth.* Chapel Hill: North Carolina, 1942. Changes made in *The Prelude* demonstrate not changes in attitude, but, rather, changes in stylistic emphases.

Bush, Douglas. *Mythology and the Romantic Tradition in English Poetry.* Cambridge: Harvard University Press, 1937. An area of study of

Wordsworth probably too often neglected. Bush can help to remedy the neglect.

Coleridge, Samuel Taylor. *Biographia Literaria; or Biographical Sketches of My Literary Life and Opinions.* London: Fenner, 1817. Analysis of Wordsworth's weaknesses and strengths by his close associate and friend.

Danby, John F. *The Simple Wordsworth: Studies in the Poems 1797-1807.* London: Routledge, 1960; New York: Barnes and Noble, 1961. Close exegetical reading of poems.

Darbishire, Helen. *The Poet Wordsworth.* The Clark Lectures, Trinity College, Cambridge, 1949. Oxford: Clarendon, 1950. Very pleasant reading. A good introduction to the poet in about 175 small pages.

Davis, Jack, ed. *William Wordsworth.* Boston: Health, 1963. "Discussions of Literature" Series. A paperback book that collects articles from good sources. A broad swath of critical opinion.

Dodds, Annie E. *The Romantic Theory of Poetry. An Examination in the Light of Croce's Aesthetic.* London: Edward Arnold and Company, 1926. Books of this kind, however questionable, can shed interesting new light.

Dunklin, Gilbert T., ed. *Wordsworth: Centenary Studies Presented at Cornell and Princeton Universities.* Princeton University Press, 1951. Articles by seven champions. The book includes papers by such experts as Douglas Bush, John Crowe Ransom, Lionel Trilling.

Elton, Oliver. *A Survey of English Literature: 1780-1830.* 2 Volumes London: The Macmillan Company, 1926. A useful volume for seeing Wordsworth in relationship to his contemporaries.

Fairchild, H. N. *Religious Trends in English Poetry,* Vol. III 1780-1830 Romantic Faith. New York: Columbia University Press, 1949. On the whole a very disappointing volume, considering the level of achievement maintained in the other volumes in the work. Prejudiced against the Romantics.

Fairchild, H. N. *The Romantic Quest.* New York: Columbia University Press, 1931. A book that students of the Movement consider basic.

Ferry, David. *The Limits of Mortality: An Essay on Wordsworth's Major Poems.* Middletown: Wesleyan University Press, 1959. One of the most suggestive of recent books on Wordsworth. Written in an unpretentious style, this book is most valuable for its revelations of Wordsworth's complex involvements with bowers, butterflies, birds. This insightful essay should help librarians and other cloistered persons to get beyond the notion that Wordsworth was loving nature every minute of his sweet-tempered life.

Havens, Raymond Dexter. *The Mind of a Poet: A Study of Wordsworth's Thought with Particular Reference to The Prelude.* Baltimore: Johns Hopkins, 1941. The serious student of Wordsworth will find here copious detail. Biography through poetry.

Hirsch, E. D., Jr. *Wordsworth and Schelling: A Typological Study of Romanticism.* New Haven: Yale. 1960. Yale Studies in English, Vol. 145. Wordsworth and Schelling found their enthusiasm independently of each other's influence.

Hough, Graham. *The Romantic Poets.* New York: W. W. Norton and Company, Inc., 1964. Needing expansion through other studies, but interesting and helpful as a summary.

Jones, John (Henry). *The Egotistical Sublime: A History of Wordsworth's Imagination.* London: Chatto and Windus, 1954. Most persons who have read this book have commented favorably. It is particularly important for its comments on Wordsworth's style. A study of stages in Wordsworth's work.

Knight, Wilson, G. *The Starlit Dome: Studies in the Poetry of Vision.* London: Oxford, 1941; re-issued London: Methuen, 1959. Knight has a gift for provocation. His ideas need the balance of less imaginative criticism, but other criticism very much needs his provocation.

Kroeber, Karl. *The Artifice of Reality: Poetic Style in Words-Worth, Foscolo, Keats, and Leopardi.* Madison and Milwaukee: Wisconsin, 1964. Kroeber discusses Romanticism as a cultural phenomenon, but not without anchoring his opinions in the cement of close critical reading of several selected poems. Careful.

Leavis, F. R. *Re-evaluation: Tradition and Development in English Poetry.* London: Chatto and Windus, 1936. Leavis had been given frequent cheers for his independent mind.

Lindenberger, Herbert. *On Wordsworth's Prelude.* Princeton University Press, 1963. One of the best available books on *The Prelude.* Lindenberger does not leave a mountain unturned.

Lyon, Judson Stanley. *The Excursion: A Study.* New Haven: Yale, 1950. Yale Studies in English, Vol. 114. A study that encompasses nearly every aspect of the poem.

Miles, Josephine. *Wordsworth and the Vocabulary of Emotion.* Berkeley and Los Angeles: California, 1942. University of California Publications in English, Vol. 12, No. 1. As the title suggests, this is a study of Wordsworth's style. A sensitive study, it makes use of statistics in its analysis of style.

Noyes, Russell. *English Romantic Poetry and Prose.* New York: Oxford University Press, 1956. This is a big anthology, big enough to include most of Wordsworth's important poetry. The spacious layout of print on the pages makes it a much more readable book than the Scott, Foresman anthology. The student should, however, find more dependable introductions than appear at the beginning of each section.

Perkins, David. *Wordsworth and the Poetry of Sincerity.* Cambridge, Mass., Harvard, 1964. This is an inclusive introduction to Wordsworth. Touches on many important subjects.

Piper, Herbert Walter. *The Active Universe: Pantheism and the Concept of the Imagination in the English Romantic Poets.* London: Athlone (Univ. of London), 1962. The Excursion is a focus of this study.

Potts, Abbie Findlay. *Wordsworth's Prelude: A Study of Its Literary Form.* Ithaca: Cornell, 1953. What Wordsworth borrowed or adapted from the 18th century is examined here. The various manuscripts of the poem are analyzed closely.

Read, Herbert. *The True Voice of Feeling: Studies in English Romantic Poetry.* London: Faber and Faber, 1953. The author concentrates on Wordsworth's meter and examines the subject of morality in his poetry.

Stallknecht, Newton P. *Strange Seas of Thought: Studies in William Wordsworth's Philosophy of Man and Nature.* Durham: Duke, 1945. The influence of Jakob Boehme on Wordsworth is considered.

Trilling, Lionel. *The Liberal Imagination.* New York: Doubleday, 1953. Wordsworth's growing awareness of the reality of death widened his vision and made it more tragic and mature. The book includes Trilling's famous essay on the "Ode."

Trilling, Lionel. *The Opposing Self.* New York: The Viking Press, 1955. There is a chapter on Wordsworth that suggests the Wordsworthian quietude as a good corrective to our modern sensibility with its preference for the apocalyptic and charismatic.

Willey, Basil. *The Seventeenth-Century Background.* London: Chatto and Windus, 1934. A chapter is included on "Wordsworth and the Locke Tradition."

Willey, Basil. *The Eighteenth-Century Background.* London: Chatto and Windus, 1940. The final chapter in a book that has nature as its central subject treats particularly Wordsworth's view of nature and suggests its value to modern readers.

Woodring, Carl, R. *Politics in the Poetry of Coleridge.* Madison: The University of Wisconsin Press, 1961. This very learned book on Coleridge can give the student insights into the Wordsworth-Coleridge relationship through a persevering study of Coleridge's concerns at the time he and Wordsworth were closely associated.

Woodring, Carl, R. *Wordsworth.* Boston: Houghton Mifflin Company, 1965. A book of very great merit, which gives highly informed introductions to poems, summaries of poems, perspicacious criticism of poems that takes in what was said before and adds new polish to the critical lens. Mr. Woodring's studies always include fact in interpretation, an invaluable assistance to the student in a time when critical readings of poems have forgotten history. A lot of education here for around $2.00.

The Ecclesiastical **Sonnets** *of William Wordsworth: A Critical Edition*, ed. Abbie Findlay Potts. New Haven: Yale, 1922. Cornell Studies in English. This book has both historical and critical helps for the student. "The Ecclesiastical Sonnets" were written in Wordsworth's later career.

The White Doe of Rylstone, *By William Wordsworth: A Critical Edition,* ed. Alice Pattee Comparetti. Ithaca: Cornell, 1940. *Cornell Studies in English,* No. 29. The book follows much the same format as the one above; it possesses the same sensitivity and accuracy.

Worthington, Jane (later Mrs. Smyser). *Wordsworth's Reading of Roman Prose.* New Haven: Yale, 1964. Yale Studies in English, Vol. 102. Perhaps because he was overshadowed by S. T. Coleridge's encyclopedic reading, it has been too easy to forget that Wordsworth read books also. Mrs. Smyser concentrates on Wordsworth's reading.

BIBLIOGRAPHIES

Healey, George Harris, ed. *The Cornell Wordsworth Collection: A Catalogue.* Ithaca: Cornell, 1957.

Henley, Elton F., and Stam, David H., eds. *Wordsworthian Criticism,* 1945-1964: An Annotated Bibliography. New York: New York Public Library, 1965.

Logan, James Venable. *Wordsworthian Criticism: A Guide and Bibliography.* Columbus: Ohio State, 1947. Granduate Monographs in Languages and Literature, No. 12.

For a more detailed listing of books and articles on Wordsworth, the interested reader will wish to consult the annual bibliography of the Romantic Movement published in *Philological Quarterly,* now published in the October issue. Up until 1962 this bibliography appeared in the April number. Before that time the bibliography of the Romantic Movement was published in the March issue of the *Journal of English Literary History.*

The following sources may also be found useful:

(1) Volume III of *The Cambridge Bibliography of English Literature,* 1940, with its Supplement of 1957.

(2) Thomas. M. Raysor, ed. *The English Romantic Poets: A Review of Research,* (New York: Modern Language Association, 1950, revised 1956).

(3) The annual bibliographies in *PMLA* and in the *Modern Humanities Research Association's Annual Bibliography of English Language and Literature.*

(4) *The Year's Work in English Studies*, published by the English Association.

(5) The Autumn issue of *Studies in English Literature.*

CONCORDANCE

Cooper, Lane, ed. *A Concordance to the Poems of William Wordsworth*. New York: Dutton; London: Smith, Elder, 1911.

www.ingramcontent.com/pod-product-compliance
Lightning Source LLC
LaVergne TN
LVHW021712060526
838200LV00050B/2625